CAKES & BAKES

CAKES & BAKES

Classic step-by-step Cookery Collection

GINA STEER
COOKERY EDITOR OF WOMAN'S OWN

HAMLYN

Contents

Family Cakes & Bakes   6

Special Occasion Cakes   22

Small Cakes & Bakes   46

Biscuits & Bakes   66

Cheesecakes & Tarts   84

First published 1992
Hamlyn is an imprint of
Octopus Illustrated Publishing,
part of Reed International Books Limited,
Michelin House, 81 Fulham Road,
London, SW3 6RB

Text and illustrations © 1992 IPC
Magazines Limited
Design © 1992 Reed International
Books Limited

All rights reserved. No part of this publication may be reproduced, stored in a retrieval system, or transmitted in any form or by any means, electronic, mechanical, photocopying, recording or otherwise, without the prior permission of the publisher.

A catalogue record for this book is available from the British Library

ISBN 0 600 57565 9

Produced by Mandarin Offset
Printed and Bound in Hong Kong

Notes

Both metric and imperial measurements have been used in all recipes.
Use one set of measurements only and not a mixture of both.

Standard level spoon measurements are used in all recipes
1 tablespoon = one 15 ml spoon
1 teaspoon = one 5 ml spoon

Ovens should be preheated to the specific temperature.
If using a fan assisted oven, follow manufacturer's instructions
for adjusting the temperature.

Introduction

This book brings together a range of cakes and bakes that will make your repertoire of recipes complete. The thought of afternoon tea brings back the memories of childhood, coming home after school, starving, or Sunday tea-time, gathered round a trolley laden with delectable fancies, and who can resist the smell of baking wafting from the kitchen? The pleasure of seeing a tray of freshly baked biscuits or pastries has a charm all of its own.

Many people feel that baking is difficult, this is not so, take the Victoria Sandwich, a true masterpiece. It's simple to make, does not use expensive and unavailable ingredients, yet provides the perfect answer for that unexpected visitor or to keep the family going in between meals.

If you want a cut-and-come-again cake, you won't go far wrong with the Cherry and Date Cake and for that extra special occasion when you're out to impress, try the Chocolate Caraque Cake – so stunning you'll have to hide it away if you want to keep it for longer than a day.

Then there are Chelsea Buns, Danish Pastries, Chocolate Brownies, Treacle Tart and a Christmas Cake to name but a few, all easy to make thanks to our clear and concise instructions and step-by-step photographs which are included in every recipe.

All the recipes in this book have been thoroughly tested in the *Woman's Own* test kitchen, so you know that you can cook each and every one of them with the sure knowledge that they will work perfectly every time and will look as good as they taste.

I hope you enjoy the book.

Happy cooking

Gina Steer

Gina Steer

BATTENBURG CAKE

Deliciously light and fluffy sponge, half flavoured with chocolate, and wrapped in marzipan, makes this cake irresistible. Follow this easy step-by-step guide and bake the family a real tea-time treat.

Calories per portion: 656 | Cuts into 15 slices

12 oz/350 g butter
   or margarine
12 oz/350 g caster sugar
6 eggs, size 3, beaten
12 oz/350 g self-raising
   flour, sieved
1 oz/25 g cocoa powder
12 oz/350 g apricot jam
2 tbsp lemon juice
1 lb/450 g white marzipan
little extra caster sugar

Preheat oven to Gas 5, 375°F, 190°C, 10 mins before baking. Line a 10 in × 7½ in/25 cm × 19 cm baking tin with lightly greased greaseproof paper. Make a partition down the centre of the tin with greaseproof paper. Lightly brush with a little cooking oil. Cream the butter or margarine with the sugar until light and fluffy. Add eggs a little at a time, with 1 tbsp of flour after each addition. Beat well. Add the remaining flour and fold in using a metal spoon to form a soft dropping consistency.

Place half the mixture into one side of the prepared tin and smooth the top. Sift the cocoa powder into the remaining mixture and fold in. If necessary, add 1-2 tbsp of cooled boiled water to form a smooth, dropping consistency. Place into the other half of the prepared tin and smooth top. Bake for 45-50 mins or until cooked and the mixture springs back when lightly pressed with fingertip. Remove from oven and leave until cold before discarding the lining paper.

Cut both of the sponges in half lengthways. If necessary, trim the halves so that all four sections are equal. Heat the jam with the lemon juice then rub through a sieve. Brush one side of a white section and one side of a chocolate section with sieved jam. Press firmly together. Brush the base and one side of the other chocolate section with jam and place on top of white sponge. Repeat with remaining white section and place on top of chocolate sponge to give a chequered effect. Press cake firmly together.

Roll marzipan out to an oblong 12 in × 9 in/30 cm × 23 cm on a lightly sugared surface. Trim edges if necessary. Brush base of cake with jam, place in centre of marzipan. Brush cake completely with jam then fold the marzipan up the sides and over the top of the cake. Press the sides firmly. Press the join firmly together and smooth by rolling lightly with a rolling pin. Turn over so join is underneath.

Make a decorative pattern along the top outside edges of the marzipan and mark diagonal lines across the top. Dust the top of the cake lightly with a little caster sugar.

HANDY TIP

If liked, food colouring can be used to colour the different sections of the cake. Allow 2 tsp of food colouring for half the basic mixture. The colour will fade when the cake is cooked.

1. Line the tin with greased greaseproof paper, dividing it in half lengthways

2. Place plain sponge mixture in one half. Add cocoa to the mixture in the bowl

3. Cut cooled sponges in half lengthways to give four equal-sized sections

CAKES & BAKES 7

4. Brush sections with jam and press together to give a chequered effect

5. Place cake in centre of the rolled-out marzipan and brush with jam

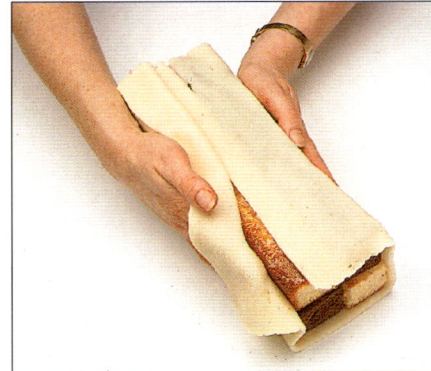

6. Press marzipan firmly around cake then turn over so join is underneath

Cherry & Date Cake

This delicious cake is guaranteed to be a family favourite. It's crammed full of cherries and dates and sprinkled with flaked almonds. The ground almonds help the cake keep its wonderful moist texture.

Calories per portion: 253 **Cuts into 12 slices**

- 4 oz/100 g glacé cherries
- 6 oz/175 g fresh dates
- 4 oz/100 g butter or margarine
- 4 oz/100 g caster sugar
- 3 eggs, size 3
- 6 oz/175 g self-raising flour
- 2 oz/50 g ground almonds
- ½ tsp almond essence
- 1 oz/25 g flaked almonds
- 2 tsp caster or granulated sugar for dredging

Preheat oven to Gas 4, 350°F, 180°C, 10 mins before baking. Grease and line the base and sides (if not using a non-stick cake tin) of a 7 in/18 cm deep cake tin with lightly oiled greaseproof paper.

Wash the cherries and roughly chop. Wash again to remove all the syrup then dry thoroughly. Wash the dates and pit, then chop roughly. Place the fat and sugar in a mixing bowl then using a wooden spoon, beat the ingredients together until they are pale and creamy. Beat the eggs and sift the flour. Add the egg a little at a time to the creamed mixture together with 1 tbsp of flour. (This will help to prevent the mixture curdling which can result in a heavy, close-textured cake.) Once all the egg has been added stir in half the flour using a metal spoon. Add the chopped cherries and the dates and fold in carefully. Add the remaining flour, the ground almonds and almond essence and gently fold into the mixture. Turn the mixture into the prepared cake tin and sprinkle the top with the flaked almonds and 1 tsp caster sugar or granulated sugar. Bake in the oven for 1 hr or until cooked. To test if the cake is cooked, insert a clean skewer into the centre of the cake, leave for approximately 10 seconds, then remove. If the skewer comes out clean the cake is cooked. Remove from oven and leave to cool in the tin. Just before serving, dredge with the remaining caster or granulated sugar.

HANDY TIP

If you cannot find fresh dates, use dried ones, look for the non sugar-coated chopped dates.

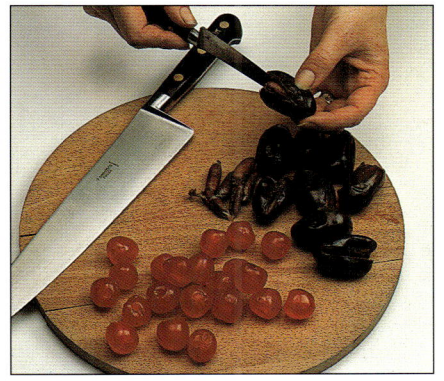

1. Wash and dry the cherries, wash and pit the dates, then chop roughly

2. Cream the fat and sugar until light and fluffy then add the eggs with 1 tbsp flour

3. Fold in cherries and dates, remaining flour, ground almonds and almond essence

4. Turn the prepared cake mixture into the greased and lined cake tin, then smooth over the top with a palette knife

5. Scatter the flaked almonds over the top of the cake and sprinkle with 1 tsp of caster or granulated sugar

6. To test if the cake is cooked, insert a clean skewer into the centre. It is cooked when it comes out clean

SWISS ROLL

When friends pop round for tea or the family fancies a home-made cake, try whisking up this easy-to-make Swiss Roll. It's light enough not to worry too much about those inches, but filling enough to keep them all happy.

Calories per portion: 252 **SERVES 6**

3 eggs, size 3
4 oz/100 g caster sugar
4 oz/100 g flour
extra caster sugar for dredging
6 tbsp whole fruit jam

Preheat oven to Gas 7, 425°F, 220°C, 15 mins before baking. Line and lightly grease a Swiss roll tin 13 in x 9 in/ 33 cm x 23 cm with a large sheet of greased greaseproof paper.

Place eggs and sugar in a large mixing bowl, place over a pan of gently simmering water and whisk until really thick and creamy. Remove from the heat and continue to whisk until cool.

Sieve the flour into the mixture then carefully fold it in, in a figure of eight movement. Then mix in 1 tbsp warm water. Pour mixture into tin, covering the whole surface evenly by tilting it gently backwards and forwards. Tap lightly on the work surface. Bake on the shelf above centre of the oven for 8-10 mins or until it's well risen, golden brown and the cake springs back when lightly touched with the fingertip.

Have ready a large sheet of greaseproof paper, liberally sprinkled with caster sugar. Place the greaseproof on a clean tea towel wrung out in hot water (this will make it easier to roll up). Turn the cooked sponge out on to the sugared greaseproof paper and remove the lining paper. Trim off the crusty edges with a sharp knife (if preferred trim when the Swiss roll is cold). Roll up the sponge and greaseproof firmly. Leave to cool.

When cold, carefully unroll. Trim edges if necessary. Gently warm the jam and stir lightly to ensure the jam is smooth. Spread the warmed jam over the Swiss roll, to within ¼ in/6 mm of edges then re-roll the sponge and dredge the top with extra sugar if liked.

Place on a serving plate.

Whisked sponges are best eaten on the day they are made; as they contain no fat, they quickly become stale.

1. Whisk mixture until it's thick and creamy and leaves a clear trail

3. Pour mixture into tin. Lightly tap on work surface to remove air pockets

5. Hold tea towel in one hand and lift slightly to make cake easier to roll

Handy Tip

For a special treat, spread 4 tbsp whipped cream on top of the jam.

2. Fold in sifted flour. Don't beat it in otherwise the sponge won't rise

4. Take care when stripping off lining paper that you don't break the sponge

6. Spread the Swiss roll with warmed, not hot, jam – using back of a spoon

Dundee Cake

Bake a cut-and-come-again cake your family and friends will all love. Filled with sultanas, currants, raisins and almonds, it's a true Scottish treat, perfect for any tea-time celebrations. It's so easy with this step-by-step recipe.

Calories per portion: 280   **Cuts into 20 slices**

- 8 oz/225 g butter or margarine
- 8 oz/225 g golden caster sugar
- 4 eggs, size 3, beaten
- 11 oz/325 g self-raising flour
- 3 oz/75 g ground almonds
- 1 orange, scrubbed and dried
- 8 oz/225 g sultanas
- 8 oz/225 g currants
- 6 oz/175 g raisins
- 1-2 tbsp sherry or milk
- 2 oz/50 g whole almonds, unskinned
- 1 tsp milk

Preheat the oven to Gas 4, 350°F, 180°C, 10 mins before baking. Grease and line sides of a 9 in/23 cm round x 3 in/7.5 cm deep cake tin with a double thickness of greaseproof paper. Cut out two 9 in/23 cm rounds of greaseproof paper to line base. Lightly grease the paper.

Cream the fat and caster sugar together until light and fluffy. Gradually add the eggs to the creamed mixture, beating well after each addition and adding 1 tbsp flour each time, to prevent the mixture curdling. After adding all the egg, fold in half the remaining flour and the ground almonds.

Finely grate rind from the orange and add to the creamed mixture. Squeeze out the juice and reserve. Fold the sultanas, currants and raisins into the mixture, using a metal spoon or spatula. Fold in the remaining flour and the reserved orange juice, then add sufficient sherry or milk to give a soft dropping consistency. Spoon the mixture into the prepared cake tin. Smooth the surface, making a slight hollow in the centre (when the cake rises during cooking, this will help to ensure that the top remains flat).

Put the whole almonds in a small glass bowl, pour boiling water over and leave to stand for 2 mins. Remove blanched almonds individually with a spoon and, using your thumb and forefinger, remove skins. If you find that, as the water cools, the skins are not so easy to remove, drain almonds, cover again with boiling water. Dry skinned almonds on kitchen paper, then arrange in circles on top of the cake mixture.

Brush nuts with milk, then bake cake on a shelf below centre for 1½-2 hrs, or until cooked. If the top browns too quickly, cover with a round of greaseproof paper or foil. Allow cake to cool in the tin before turning out on to wire rack.

Leave until cold, then discard the greaseproof paper and store the cake in an airtight tin.

Handy tip

This cake improves if kept 2-3 days before eating.

1. Grease a 9 in/23 cm cake tin and line the sides with a double thickness of greaseproof paper

2. Cut out two 9 in/23 cm rounds of greaseproof paper to line the base of the tin. Lightly grease the paper

3. Finely grate the rind from the orange and fold into the creamed mixture. Squeeze out the juice and reserve

CAKES & BAKES 13

4. Add dried fruit and remaining flour. Mix to dropping consistency with juice and sherry or milk. Spoon into prepared tin

5. Put whole almonds in a bowl, pour boiling water over, leave to stand for 2 mins, remove skins

6. Dry the skinned almonds, then arrange in circles on top of cake mixture. Brush with milk and bake

Walnut Cake

Light coffee-flavoured sponge, layered with a delicious French butter icing and topped with crunchy walnuts – this cake is mouthwatering. So go on, treat yourself and spoil your family and friends; you'll find one slice just won't be enough.

Calories per portion: 640   SERVES 10

- 8 oz/225 g softened butter or margarine
- 8 oz/225 g caster sugar
- 4 eggs, size 3, beaten
- 8 oz/225 g self-raising flour
- 2 tbsp liquid coffee or very strong black coffee
- 5 oz/150 g walnut halves

FOR THE ICING:
- 4 oz/100 g granulated sugar
- 2 egg yolks, size 3
- 10 oz/300 g unsalted butter
- 2 tbsp liquid coffee or very strong black coffee

Preheat oven to Gas 5, 375°F, 190°C, 10 mins before baking. Lightly grease and line the bases of two 8 in/20.5 cm sandwich tins. Cream the fat with the sugar until light and fluffy. Gradually add the eggs with a little of the flour, beating well between each addition. Stir in the coffee and ensure mixture is thoroughly mixed together. Stir in remaining flour with 2 tbsp of water to give a soft dropping consistency.

Reserve a few of the walnuts for decoration, then chop the remainder and fold into the mixture. Divide between the two prepared sandwich tins and smooth the tops.

Bake on the centre shelf for 25-30 mins, or until cooked. The cake is cooked when the top springs back if lightly pressed with the finger. Remove from the oven and leave for 5 mins to cool slightly before turning the cakes out on to a wire cooling rack. Leave until cold. Discard lining paper.

Meanwhile, make the icing. Mix the sugar with 8 fl oz/250 ml of water in a heavy-based pan. Heat gently, stirring occasionally, until sugar has dissolved. Then increase the heat and boil steadily until a sugar syrup is reached to the thread stage, or a sugar thermometer registers 220°F, 105°C. Remove from heat and pour into a glass jug. Place egg yolks in a bowl and whisk lightly, then gradually whisk in the sugar syrup. Continue to whisk until cold.

Cut butter into small pieces then gradually whisk into the mixture, whisk only small amounts in at a time – don't be tempted to add the butter all at once. When all the butter has been used, whisk in the liquid coffee. Use one quarter of the icing to sandwich the cakes together. Cover the cake completely with the remaining icing. Then, with a palette or round-bladed knife, work around the cake in a swirling pattern. Place the reserved walnut halves on top.

Handy tips

When making the icing, if you don't have a sugar thermometer, you can easily test if the syrup is ready. Dip a spoon into syrup, press another on to the back of it and pull away. If a thread is formed, the syrup is ready. To freeze sponge cakes, cook then wrap separately in clearwrap and then foil. Thaw before decorating.

1. Cream fat and sugar, beat in eggs and a little flour, add liquid coffee

2. Fold in the remaining flour. Chop the walnuts, then fold into the mixture

3. Dissolve sugar in water over a gentle heat. Boil until it's 220°F, 105°C

4. Whisk egg yolks, then whisk in sugar syrup, pouring in a thin stream

5. Whisk until cold. Add the butter, whisking well between each addition

6. Using icing, sandwich cakes together, coat whole cake and swirl with knife

Genoa Cake

Bake a cake that's quick and easy to make and simply delicious, too! A classic super-light sponge that's crammed with glacé cherries and is a treat any time of the day. Serve up a slice for a taste all the family are sure to love.

Calories per portion: 344   **Cuts into 12 slices**

- 6 oz/175 g glacé cherries
- 7 oz/200 g self-raising flour, sieved
- 6 oz/175 g butter or margarine
- 6 oz/175 g caster sugar
- 4 eggs, size 3
- 1 oz/25 g ground almonds
- 1 tbsp icing sugar

Preheat the oven to Gas 4, 350°F, 180°C, 10 mins before baking. Then place a 7 in/18 cm deep cake tin on to a double sheet of greaseproof paper, draw around the base then cut out the circle. Fold another sheet of greaseproof paper in half (the length of the paper needs to measure the same as the circumference of the tin). Brush inside the fold lightly with oil so that the paper stays together. Fold over about 1 in/2.5 cm and crease, then make diagonal cuts to the crease line at about 2 in/5 cm intervals. Lightly grease the cake tin with oil, then line the sides and base with the paper, easing it into the tin. Brush lightly with oil.

Wash the cherries thoroughly to remove syrup, then dry on kitchen paper, chop roughly, and place in a small bowl. Stir 1 tbsp flour into the cherries and toss well, until cherries are completely coated.

Place the butter or margarine in a mixing bowl, add the sugar, then beat together until light and fluffy. Beat in the eggs, one at a time, adding 1 tbsp of flour after each addition.

Using a metal spoon or spatula, stir the remaining flour into the mixture. Fold in the ground almonds and the chopped cherries. Mix lightly to distribute cherries evenly, adding, if necessary, 1-2 tbsp of tepid boiled water to give the mixture a soft dropping consistency.

Turn into the prepared tin and smooth over the top. Make a slight hollow in the centre of the mixture to allow for the cake to rise. Bake in the preheated oven for 1-1¼ hrs, or until cake is cooked.

To test whether the cake is cooked, lightly touch the top with your forefinger. If the cake springs back and feels firm to the touch, then it's ready. Remove from the oven and allow to cool in the tin for at least 10 mins before removing from the tin and discarding the lining paper. Then leave to cool on a wire cooling rack. When cold, sieve the icing sugar over the top of the cake and serve.

Handy tip

Mix together 3 oz/75 g of sieved icing sugar, strained juice of one small lemon and sufficient hot water to give a coating consistency. Spread over top of cooled cake. Decorate with extra halved glacé cherries.

1. Grease and line a 7 in/18 cm cake tin with greaseproof paper

2. Wash the cherries to remove the syrup, dry thoroughly, then chop roughly

3. Cream butter or margarine together with the sugar until light and fluffy

CAKES & BAKES 17

4. Beat the eggs one at a time, adding 1 tbsp of flour after each addition

5. Fold the cherries into cake mixture, ensuring they are well distributed

6. Spoon mixture into lined cake tin, bake in preheated oven for about 1 hr

VICTORIA SANDWICH

This simple sandwich cake proves that good cooking doesn't need flashy tricks or expensive ingredients. A deliciously light sponge cake filled with raspberry jam – it will be a favourite with all the family. So give them a treat today!

Calories per portion: 444   **Cuts into 8 slices**

Cakes & Bakes

6 oz/175 g butter or margarine
6 oz/175 g caster sugar
3 eggs, size 3, beaten
6 oz/175 g self-raising flour
3-4 tbsp raspberry jam
caster sugar for dredging

Preheat oven to Gas 4, 350°F, 180°C, 10 mins before baking. If not using non-stick sponge tins, then line bases with greased greaseproof paper. Or lightly grease the bases and sides of two 7 in/18 cm sponge tins with a little oil.

Cream the butter or margarine and sugar together until soft and fluffy. Gradually beat in the eggs, a little at a time, sifting in a little flour between each addition. This ensures that the mixture does not curdle.

Sift in the remaining flour and fold into the mixture with a metal spoon. Do not mix in vigorously. Use a cutting action to ensure that you do not destroy the air you have beaten in by the original creaming. If the mixture is too dry carefully fold in 1-2 tbsp tepid boiled water. This will keep the mixture light and fluffy. Other liquids tend to be dense and often result in a heavier sponge. The mixture should have a soft dropping consistency (when you pick the spoon up, and lightly tap on the side of the bowl the mixture should gently drop back into the bowl).

Divide the mixture evenly between each tin. A foolproof method is to weigh each tin after you have put the mixture in. Smooth over the top of the mixture and bake in the centre of the oven for 20-25 mins or until the cake is golden brown and when touched lightly with the tip of a finger, it springs back.

Turn out and cool on wire cooling racks. When cold, if necessary, remove lining paper. Sandwich the sponges together with jam and dredge the top with caster sugar.

> **Handy tip**
>
> For a change, cream 2 oz/50 g butter with 4 oz/100 g icing sugar and the grated rind of one lemon, and use as a filling.

1. Assemble and weigh the ingredients before you start to make the sponge

2. Beat the eggs, a little at a time, into creamed sugar and butter mixture

3. Sift the remaining flour into the cake mixture and fold in carefully

4. Fold in a little tepid water until the mixture is a soft dropping consistency

5. Divide the mixture between prepared cake tins and smooth the top

6. Sandwich both the cooled cakes together with the raspberry jam

Chocolate Cake

Spoil your family and friends with this delicious no-need-to-cook chocolate cake. Packed full of sun-ripened sultanas and raisins, cherries and almonds, then topped with wicked chocolate curls, every serving's a slice of heaven.

Calories per portion: 333 — **Serves 12**

- 6 oz/175 g plain chocolate
- 3 tbsp brandy, orange juice or water
- 2 oz/50 g icing sugar
- 4 oz/100 g butter, preferably unsalted, softened
- 2 egg yolks, size 3
- 2 oz/50 g glacé cherries, washed, dried and chopped
- 2 oz/50 g sultanas
- 2 oz/50 g raisins
- 2 oz/50 g chopped almonds
- 6 oz/175 g digestive biscuits
- ¼ pint/150 ml whipping cream
- chocolate curls
- 2 tsp icing sugar
- fresh fruit and cream to serve

Lightly grease an 8 in/20.5 cm loose-bottomed cake tin. Break chocolate into pieces and place in a bowl with the brandy, orange juice or water. Place over a pan of gently simmering water and stir until melted. Remove from heat and leave to cool.

Sieve icing sugar into a bowl, add butter and beat with a wooden spoon until soft and creamy. Beat in the egg yolks.

Add chopped cherries to the butter mixture together with the sultanas, raisins and almonds. Stir in cooled chocolate and mix well.

Place biscuits in a polythene bag and crush with a rolling pin until broken up into small pieces. Add to chocolate mixture and mix in well.

Lightly whip the cream and stir into the mixture. Spoon into the cake tin and smooth the top with a palette knife until level. Place in the fridge and leave overnight until firm and set.

When ready to serve rest the cake tin base on top of a clean can and gently pull the side of the cake tin down from the cake. Remove cake tin base and place cake on a serving plate. Decorate with chocolate curls and sieve a little icing sugar over the top. Serve cut into slices with fruit and cream.

Handy tips

If you're worried about using egg yolks in this recipe, they may be omitted – the cake mixture will just be slightly less rich. If preferred, you can use any other type of plain biscuit, instead of digestives.

1. Heat the chocolate with the brandy, orange juice or water until melted

2. Cream together the icing sugar and butter, then beat in the egg yolks

3. Place the biscuits in a polythene bag and crush with a rolling pin

CAKES & BAKES **21**

4. Spoon the whipped cream into the chocolate biscuit mixture and mix well

5. Smooth the mixture evenly into a greased, loose-bottomed cake tin

6. Rest cake tin base on a clean can and ease the side of the cake tin down

Yule log

This light and fluffy chocolate sponge, filled with vanilla butter cream and covered in chocolate, is a must for everyone's Christmas! It's so quick and easy to make, and so much nicer to serve a home-made cake for Christmas tea.

Calories per portion: 462 **Cuts into 8 slices**

3 eggs, size 1
4 oz/100 g caster sugar
3½ oz/90 g self-raising flour
½ oz/15 g cocoa powder
6 oz/175 g softened butter or soft margarine
12 oz/350 g icing sugar, sifted
½ tsp vanilla essence
4 oz/100 g dark chocolate

Preheat oven to Gas 7, 425°F, 220°C, 15 mins before baking. Lightly grease and line a 13 in × 9 in/32.5 cm × 23 cm Swiss roll tin with greased greaseproof paper.

Crack eggs into a large mixing bowl with sugar over a pan of gently simmering water and whisk until thick and doubled in volume. The whisk should leave a trail across top of mixture when lightly pulled across. Remove from the heat and continue to whisk until the mixture is cold.

Sift flour and cocoa powder together and gently fold into mixture in a figure of eight movement. Then fold in 1 tbsp of tepid water. Take care not to over mix or the air you have whisked in will

be knocked out. When all the flour and cocoa powder has been thoroughly incorporated pour into prepared Swiss roll tin, allowing the mixture to find its own level. Tap lightly on the surface to remove any air bubbles.

Bake on the shelf above centre for 8-10 mins or until the sponge is cooked. The top should spring back when touched lightly with the finger. Have ready a large sheet of greaseproof paper lightly sprinkled with a little caster sugar.

When sponge is cooked, remove from oven, turn out on to greaseproof paper and carefully strip away lining paper. Roll the sponge with the greaseproof paper inside. Allow to cool.

Meanwhile prepare butter cream. Cream butter or margarine until soft, then gradually beat in icing sugar, making sure there are no lumps. Beat until soft and fluffy. If necessary add a little warm water. Place 4 tbsp butter cream in a small bowl then beat in the vanilla essence.

Melt chocolate in a small bowl over a pan of gently simmering water, or in a microwave following manufacturer's instructions, stir well, then beat into remaining butter cream.

Unwrap cold Swiss roll, discard greaseproof paper, trim all edges and spread vanilla butter cream to within ¼ in/6 mm of the edge. Carefully roll up with the join underneath. Trim away both ends by ¼ in/6 mm. Cut Swiss roll diagonally in half and arrange in log shape as shown. Cover with chocolate butter cream and use a fork to mark the bark. Place on a serving board. Dust with icing sugar and decorate.

HANDY TIPS

If you have a free standing electric mixer, make Swiss roll by placing eggs and sugar in a bowl, then using the balloon whisk attachment whisk the mixture, without placing the bowl over a pan of simmering water – takes about 8-10 mins. Put 1-2 tsp granulated sugar in the buttercream for an extra crunch.
To make mini Swiss rolls, cook as before, roll up and leave until cold. Cut unrolled cake in half lengthways, then into 4 pieces (making 8 pieces in all). Cover with butter cream, roll up and coat as before.

1. Whisk the eggs and sugar over a pan of gently simmering water until thick and doubled in volume

2. Gently fold in the sifted flour and cocoa powder in a figure of eight movement. Then fold in 1 tbsp of tepid water

3. Turn the cake out on to a sugared piece of greaseproof paper. Discard the lining paper

4. Roll the Swiss roll up with the sheet of greaseproof paper and leave until cold

5. Cut the filled Swiss roll diagonally in half and place together to form the log

6. Spread log with chocolate butter cream, mark with prongs of fork for the bark

Simnel Cake

This cake was originally baked for mothers on Mothering Sunday, in the days when many girls went into service, and that was the one day they were allowed home. Now Easter wouldn't be complete without a slice of this tasty treat.

Calories per portion: 665 **Cuts into 10 slices**

10 oz/300 g self-raising flour
2 oz/50 g ground almonds
5 oz/150 g butter or margarine
5 oz/150 g caster sugar
1 lb/450 g mixed dried fruit
grated rind and juice of
    1 large lemon
5 eggs, size 3
2-3 tbsp milk
1¼ lb/550 g ready-made
    marzipan
2 tbsp apricot jam, sieved

Preheat oven to Gas 4, 350°F, 180°C, 10 mins before baking. Grease and line an 8 in/20.5 cm cake tin with greaseproof paper. Sift flour into mixing bowl and stir in ground almonds. Rub in fat until mixture resembles fine breadcrumbs. Stir in sugar, dried fruit and lemon rind. Beat the eggs and stir into mixture with lemon juice and sufficient milk to form a soft dropping consistency. Place half the mixture in cake tin and smooth the top.

Divide marzipan into three and on a surface lightly dusted with icing sugar roll out one third to an 8 in/20.5 cm round and place on top of cake mixture. Spoon remaining cake mixture over the marzipan and smooth the top.

Bake in the centre of the oven for 1¼-1½ hrs or until cooked. To test if the cake is cooked, insert a skewer into the centre of the cake and if clean when removed, the cake is cooked. Allow to cool in tin before turning out.

Shape a further third of the marzipan into small balls. Roll out the final third of the marzipan to an 8 in/20.5 cm round. Remove the greaseproof paper from the cake and brush the top with the apricot jam.

Place the marzipan circle on top of the cake and press down lightly and pinch up the sides with the forefinger and thumb to form a decorative edge. If liked place under a preheated grill for 3-5 mins turning round frequently to lightly brown on the top.

Place the marzipan balls round the edge, fixing with a little of the apricot jam. Decorate the top with Easter chicks and tie a band of ribbon round the outside of the cake to add the perfect finishing touch.

HANDY TIP

Traditionally a Simnel cake has 11 balls of marzipan to represent the Apostles minus Judas. But you can in fact decorate the cake with as many as you like. Alternatively, decorate the top with little Easter eggs.

1. Rub fat into flour and almonds until mixture resembles fine breadcrumbs

2. Stir in fruit, add eggs gradually and beat together well; stir in the lemon juice

3. On lightly sugared surface, roll out one third of marzipan to 8 in/20.5 cm round

4. Place half the prepared mixture in tin, smooth surface. Place marzipan on top

5. Allow the cake to cool, brush top with apricot jam and add marzipan circle

6. Fix the marzipan balls on top of the cake with just a little apricot jam

Angel Food Cake

Simple to make, heavenly to eat, this luscious cake is a perfect tea-time treat, especially for those with a sweet tooth! Coated with a sugary frosting, it's so light, you can even indulge in a second slice.

Calories per portion: 202   Serves 12

FOR THE CAKE:
plain flour for dusting
3 oz/75 g plain flour
6 oz/175 g caster sugar
5 egg whites, size 3
1 tsp cream of tartar
pinch of salt
½ tsp vanilla essence
¼ tsp almond essence

FOR THE FROSTING:
12 oz/350 g caster sugar
2 egg whites, size 3
pinch each of cream of tartar and salt
dried rose petals, lemon-scented geranium leaves and grapes, all lightly washed, and dried for decoration

Preheat the oven to Gas 4, 350°F, 180°C, 10 mins before baking. Lightly dust a 2½ pint/1.5 litre ungreased ring mould with a little plain flour.

Sieve the flour and half of the sugar six times. This helps to aerate the ingredients and ensures a light texture. Whisk the egg whites until softly peaking, then whisk in the cream of tartar, salt, vanilla and almond essences, until thoroughly incorporated. Gradually add remaining half of the sugar, whisking well after each addition, until fully incorporated. The mixture should be stiff and standing in peaks by this time.

When all the sugar has been added, sieve in one third of the flour and sugar mixture, and fold in carefully using a spatula or metal spoon – add half the remaining flour and sugar, sieving and folding it in.. Repeat once more. Spoon the mixture into the prepared ring mould, then tap lightly on the surface and smooth the top. Bake in the oven for 30-40 mins or until cooked – the top should spring back when lightly touched with a finger.

Remove from the oven and invert on to a wire cooling rack. Leave until cold then remove mould. (On cooling the mixture retracts slightly and the mould can easily be removed.) If necessary, gently ease the cake away with the tip of a round-bladed knife.

To prepare the frosting, place a large bowl over a pan of gently simmering water and allow to warm. Remove bowl from pan and place caster sugar, egg whites, cream of tartar and salt in the bowl. Add 4 tbsp of water and whisk until well blended. Turn off heat, then replace bowl over pan and whisk until mixture forms soft peaks.

Place the cake the right way up on a serving plate and cover with frosting. Decorate with rose petals, geranium leaves and grapes, or any other decoration of your choice. Carefully wipe round edge of cake to remove any frosting on plate. Leave until set.

Handy tip

Try crystallizing the decoration: brush the leaves and grapes lightly with beaten egg white, coat in caster sugar and leave to dry.

1. Sieve the flour and the sugar six times. This will ensure a light texture

2. Whisk egg whites until peaking, add cream of tartar, salt and essences

3. Whisk in half the sugar, ensuring each addition is thoroughly incorporated

Cakes & Bakes

4. Sieve a third of the flour and sugar mixture into egg whites and fold in

5. Spoon into a clean, ungreased ring mould, tap lightly to level top

6. After baking leave on wire cooking rack until cold. Carefully remove mould

PASSION CAKE

Show the one you love that you really care by making this special cake for Valentine's Day. Wonderfully moist, it has a superb light texture and a delicious butter and crème fraîche filling, subtly flavoured with passion fruit juice.

Calories per portion: 502   Cuts into 12 slices

6 oz/175 g butter or margarine
6 oz/175 g light soft brown sugar
3 eggs, size 3
10 oz/300 g self-raising flour
2 oz/50 g walnut pieces
6 oz/175 g carrots, peeled
    and grated
FOR THE FROSTING:
2 oz/50 g unsalted butter
2 fl oz/50 ml crème fraîche
12 oz/350 g icing sugar, sifted
2 passion fruit
3 oz/75 g walnut pieces,
    finely chopped
1 oz/25 g dark chocolate, melted

Preheat oven to Gas 5, 375°F, 190°C, 10 mins before baking. Grease and line with greased greaseproof paper, bases of two 7 in/18 cm sandwich cake tins.

Cream butter or margarine with sugar in a bowl until light and fluffy. Beat eggs, then gradually beat into creamed mixture with 1-2 tbsp of flour to prevent the mixture curdling. Fold in remaining flour using a metal spoon or spatula, with 3-4 tbsp warm water to form a soft dropping consistency. Chop walnuts finely then mix into cake with grated carrot. Divide between cake tins, smoothing over top.

Bake on centre shelf for 30-35 mins or until mixture springs back when lightly touched with a clean finger. Remove from oven, leave to cool for 5 mins. Turn on to wire cooling rack. Leave until cold. Discard the lining paper.

To make the frosting: beat the butter with the crème fraîche then gradually beat in 8 oz/225 g icing sugar.

Cut the passion fruits in half, scoop out the seeds into a fine sieve then press out the juice. Use 1-2 tbsp to flavour frosting. Sandwich the cold cake together with a little of the frosting.

Spread the outside edge with frosting then, holding the cake firmly

HANDY TIP

Passion fruit are ripe when the skins are soft and wrinkled. You can also use other flavourings in the frosting. Try orange, lemon, vanilla or, for a special treat, brandy.

with both hands, roll in the chopped walnuts until the sides are thoroughly coated. Place on serving plate.

Put remaining frosting in a piping bag fitted with a small star nozzle and pipe small rosettes around the edge of the cake. Mix the remaining icing sugar with the remaining passion fruit juice and a little water if necessary to form a smooth icing, then carefully flood the top of the cake, allowing the icing to find its own level. Allow to set completely before piping the wording of your choice with melted chocolate.

1. Before starting to make the cake, finely chop the walnuts and grate the carrot

2. Cream butter and light soft brown sugar together until fluffy. Beat in eggs

3. After folding in flour, carefully mix in grated carrot and then chopped walnuts

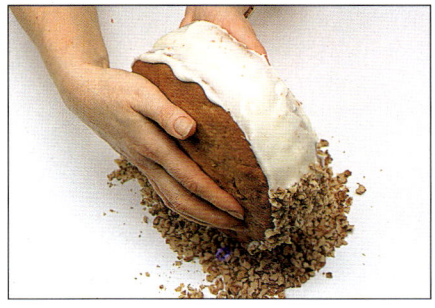

4. Divide mixture between prepared cake tins; smooth top with palette knife

5. Sandwich cakes together, spread frosting around edges, coat with walnuts

6. Place frosting in piping bag fitted with star nozzle and pipe rosettes on cake

Christmas Cake

Bake a wonderfully rich and moist cake, packed full of luscious fruits, cherries and nuts. Traditionally iced and decorated, all your family and friends will want slice after slice of this Christmas treat – and it's so simple to make.

Calories per portion: 586

Makes 9 in/13 cm round cake

1. Make the cake mixture, spoon into a greased, lined cake tin and smooth top

2. Warm jam and lemon juice, pass through a sieve, then use to glaze cake

3. Roll out almond paste into two strips, place around cake and trim sides

- 12 oz/350 g butter or margarine
- 12 oz/350 g light soft brown sugar
- 5 eggs, size 3, beaten
- 10 oz/300 g plain flour
- 4 oz/100 g ground almonds
- ½ tsp ground cinnamon
- ½ tsp ground ginger
- ½ tsp ground cloves
- ½ tsp freshly grated nutmeg
- 1 tbsp black treacle, warmed
- grated rind and juice of 1 lemon
- 10 oz/300 g sultanas
- 10 oz/300 g seedless raisins
- 6 oz/175 g currants
- 3 oz/75 g chopped mixed nuts
- 3 oz/75 g glacé cherries, washed, dried and chopped
- approx 1½ tbsp brandy or fruit juice

FOR THE ALMOND PASTE:
- 12 oz/350 g ground almonds
- 6 oz/175 g caster sugar
- 6 oz/175 g icing sugar, sieved
- 2 eggs, size 5, beaten
- ½ tsp vanilla essence
- ½ tsp almond essence

FOR THE APRICOT GLAZE:
- 1 tbsp apricot jam
- 2 tsp lemon juice

FOR THE ROYAL ICING:
- 3 egg whites, size 3
- 1½ lb/675 g icing sugar, sifted
- 1 tbsp lemon juice
- 1-2 tsp glycerine

Preheat the oven to Gas 2, 300°F, 150°C, 15 mins before baking. Grease and line a 9 in/23 cm round cake tin with four layers of greaseproof paper.

Cream the fat and sugar until light and fluffy, then beat in the eggs, adding 1 tbsp of flour after each addition. Add the ground almonds, together with the spices and black treacle. Mix well. Stir in half the remaining flour with the lemon rind and juice, dried fruit, nuts and cherries. Stir thoroughly. Add the remaining flour with the brandy or fruit juice, to give a soft dropping consistency. Turn mixture into prepared cake tin and smooth the top. Make a slight hollow in the centre to ensure a flat cake. Bake towards the bottom of the oven for 2 hrs, then reduce the oven temperature to Gas 1, 275°F, 140°C, and cook the cake for a further 1½-2 hrs, or until a skewer inserted into the centre comes out clean. If the top is browning too quickly, cover with greaseproof paper. When cooked, remove from the oven and leave in the tin until cold. Remove from tin, store wrapped in greaseproof paper, then foil in a cool, dry place. If liked, prick with a skewer and pour 1-2 tbsp brandy over.

When ready to decorate, discard lining paper. If necessary, trim cake.

Mix the ground almonds and sugars in a bowl, stir in sufficient egg to make a soft but not wet consistency, then add the essences and knead until smooth. Wrap in clearwrap.

Heat the jam and lemon juice together, rub through a sieve. Cool, use to glaze surface of cake.

Reserve a third of the almond paste, then divide the remainder into two. On a lightly sugared surface roll each piece into a strip the depth of the cake and half the circumference. Place around sides of cake, trim and press firmly. Roll out remaining almond paste into a round the same size as the cake. Place on top of cake. Smooth top and sides using a rolling pin, place on a cake board and leave to dry for three days.

Whisk egg whites until lightly stiff, then whisk in the icing sugar a little at a time. If the mixture becomes too stiff, add a little of the lemon juice. Whisk in the glycerine. The mixture should be stiff enough for you to form soft peaks with a knife. Cover cake completely. Then make small swirls with a palette knife over the whole cake. Decorate, then leave to set for at least two days.

HANDY TIP

For a change, decorate the cake with glacé fruit and nuts. Omit the almond paste and royal icing, brush the top of the cake with apricot glaze and decorate with fruit and nuts.

4. Roll remaining almond paste into a round the size of a cake top, position

5. Spoon prepared royal icing on to cake, using palette knife cover completely

6. Ensure the icing is of uniform depth, then make swirls all over the cake

STOLLEN

This delicious bread is a great German classic, full of moist cherries, sultanas, apricots and nuts, with a hint of spice. Encased is a mouthwatering layer of marzipan, bake it for a tasty change.

Calories per portion: 387　　**Each loaf cuts into 12 slices**

3 oz/75 g glacé cherries
3 oz/75 g dried apricots
4 oz/100 g sultanas
2 oz/50 g mixed peel
¼ pint/150 ml rum, optional
3 oz/75 g flaked almonds
grated rind of 1 lemon
3 eggs, size 3
½ pint/300 ml milk
2 x ½ oz/15 g sachets dried yeast
8 oz/225 g golden caster sugar
8 oz/225 g butter, cut into small pieces
2 lb/900 g strong white flour
2 tsp ground cinnamon
12 oz/350 g white marzipan
2 tbsp icing sugar, sieved

Preheat the oven to Gas 6, 400°F, 200°C, 15 mins before baking. Lightly grease two baking sheets. Wash and dry the cherries. Chop cherries and apricots roughly. Put the chopped fruit in separate small bowls, and the sultanas and mixed peel in another. Heat rum, if using, and add ¼ pint/150 ml tepid water. Pour over fruits and leave to soak for at least 2 hrs. (If not using rum, use ½ pint/300 ml tepid water.)

Drain fruits, then mix together. Add the flaked almonds and grated lemon rind. Reserve. Place eggs in large bowl and beat thoroughly.

Heat milk to blood heat, add dried yeast and a pinch of caster sugar. Leave in a warm place for 15 mins until frothy. Heat remaining sugar with the butter. Stir until sugar has dissolved and butter has melted. Remove from heat, add to yeast mixture, then pour over the eggs, beating well.

Sieve flour into large bowl, then stir half into the egg mixture, together with the cinnamon. Mix well, then cover and leave in a warm place for 1 hr, or until mixture has risen and is spongy. Add remaining flour to mixture, mix well, then turn out on to a lightly floured surface and knead until smooth.

Add prepared fruits and nuts, and knead until fully incorporated.

Halve dough and roll out to form an oblong. Roll out half the marzipan to a thin oblong, about a quarter of the size of the dough, and place in centre. Fold edges of dough over, then roll up, completely encasing marzipan. Shape ends to form a neat oval. Repeat with remaining dough and marzipan.

Place on baking sheets, cover with a tea towel, then leave to rise for about 1 hr. Bake in oven for 15 mins, then reduce temperature to Gas 4, 350°F, 180°C, and bake for a further 1-1¼ hrs, or until cooked. (The loaves should sound hollow when tapped lightly on the base.)

Remove from oven and dust with the icing sugar. Eat within 24 hrs.

Handy tip

If liked freeze until required, warming through gently after thawing.

1. Chop the cherries. Soak the fruit, drain, then add almonds and lemon rind

2. Beat the eggs in a large bowl, then pour in the yeast and butter mixture

3. Sieve the flour into a large bowl. Gradually stir half into the egg mixture

4. Coat the sides of the cake with whipped cream, then roll in the toasted mixed nuts

5. Transfer cake to a serving plate, then pipe rosettes of cream around the top of the cake

6. Arrange the fruit on top of the cake, then glaze with the cooled redcurrant jelly. Serve with cream

Devil's Food Cake

Bake a truly wicked treat with this really mouthwatering classic American recipe. A rich, moist chocolate sponge, covered in a tasty fudge icing, this cake is sure to become an all-time favourite.

Calories per portion: 473   CUTS INTO 12 SLICES

1. Break the chocolate into pieces, place in heavy-based pan with yogurt and 3 oz/75 g brown sugar

2. Cream fat with remaining sugar until light and fluffy. Beat in eggs with a little flour and cocoa powder

3. Stir cooled chocolate mixture into creamed ingredients, stir lightly together. Add sifted flour and cocoa

Cakes & Bakes

- 3 oz/75 g plain chocolate
- ¼ pint/150 ml low-fat natural yogurt
- 7 oz/200 g light soft brown sugar
- 4 oz/100 g butter or margarine
- 4 eggs, size 3
- 8 oz/225 g self-raising flour, sifted
- 2 tbsp cocoa powder, sifted

FOR THE FUDGE ICING:
- 12 oz/350 g icing sugar
- 2 tbsp cocoa powder
- 4-6 tbsp semi-skimmed milk
- 2 oz/50 g plain chocolate
- 2½ oz/65 g white vegetable fat

Preheat the oven to Gas 4, 350°F, 180°C, 10 mins before cooking. Grease two 7 in/18 cm sandwich tins, line bases with greaseproof paper.

Break the chocolate into small pieces, place in a heavy-based pan with the yogurt and 3 oz/75 g of the brown sugar. Place over a gentle heat and warm the mixture through, stirring occasionally, until chocolate has melted. Remove from heat, allow to cool. Cream remaining sugar and fat together until light and fluffy, then beat in the eggs one at a time, adding a little of the sifted flour and cocoa powder after each egg.

Once the chocolate mixture has cooled, add to the creamed ingredients and stir lightly together. Then add the remaining flour and cocoa powder. Mix lightly together until blended, then divide between the lined sandwich tins, smooth tops with a palette knife and bake in the oven for 25-35 mins, or until cooked. When ready, the top of each cake will spring back if touched lightly with the finger. Remove both cakes from oven and leave for 5 mins before turning out on to wire cooling racks. Leave until both the cakes are cold before beginning the icing.

To make the icing, sift the icing sugar and the cocoa powder together. Place 4 tbsp of the milk, the chocolate broken into small pieces and the white vegetable fat into a small pan. Place the pan over a gentle heat and stir the ingredients until they have melted and blended together. Remove from the heat, then stir into the sifted icing sugar and cocoa powder. Beat the mixture thoroughly with a wooden spoon, until the icing is smooth, thick and of a spreadable consistency, adding extra milk if required.

Discard the lining paper from the cold sponges, sandwich them together with a third of the prepared icing. Use remaining icing to cover the top and sides of the cake, swirling with a palette knife to create a decorative effect. Allow at least 2 hrs for icing to set before cutting.

Handy tip

For a change try a mocha icing: simply add 2 tbsp strong black coffee to the chocolate and white vegetable fat. Use only 2-4 tbsp of milk, when making the icing.

4. For the icing, mix the melted chocolate mixture into the sifted icing sugar and cocoa. Beat until thick and smooth

5. Discard lining paper from cakes. Spread prepared icing over one of the cooled cakes, place the other on top

6. Place the remaining icing on top of the cake, then swirl over the top and sides with a palette knife to decorate

Chocolate Caraque Cake

A Sachertorte is the ultimate chocolate cake. The original recipe, created in Vienna is a closely guarded secret, but this recipe is equally delicious.

Calories per portion: 539 **Serves 12**

1. Cream the butter and sugar together until light and fluffy, beat in the egg yolks then the cooled chocolate

2. Discard lining paper, place on cooling rack. Brush the sides and top of the cake, once cold, with the sieved apricot jam

3. Make the chocolate icing and leave for 20 mins until cold or until thickened slightly, then pour over the cake

Cakes & Bakes

FOR THE CAKE:
8 oz/225 g plain dark chocolate
6 oz/175 g unsalted butter
6 oz/175 g caster sugar
6 eggs, size 3
1 oz/25 g ground almonds
5 oz/150 g self-raising flour
FOR THE ICING:
2 tbsp apricot jam
6 oz/175 g plain dark chocolate
3 oz/75 g unsalted butter
2 tsp golden syrup
FOR THE CARAQUE CURLS:
4 oz/100 g plain dark chocolate

Preheat the oven to Gas 4, 350°F, 180°C, 10 mins before baking the cake. Grease and line the base of an 8 in/20.5 cm loose-bottomed springform tin with greaseproof paper. (If not using a non-stick cake tin, grease and line the sides as well.) Break the chocolate into small pieces, place in a small bowl and stand over a pan of gently simmering water, stirring occasionally and allow the chocolate to melt. Remove the bowl from the pan and leave to cool.

Cream the butter and sugar together until light and fluffy. Separate the eggs then beat in the egg yolks one at a time, then beat in the cooled chocolate. Add the ground almonds then sieve the flour and stir into the mixture with 3 tbsp tepid boiled water.

Whisk the egg whites until stiff then gradually stir into the cake mixture. When all the egg whites have been thoroughly incorporated, turn the mixture into the prepared tin. Tap the tin lightly on the work surface to remove any air bubbles.

Bake in the oven for 40-45 mins or until a skewer inserted into the centre comes out clean. Remove from the tin and allow to become cold before removing from the tin.

Warm the apricot jam then sieve. Discard the lining paper from the cake then place on a wire cooling rack placed over a large plate. Brush the top and sides with the sieved apricot jam.

Make the icing by breaking the chocolate into small pieces and placing in a heavy-based saucepan with the butter and golden syrup. Place over a gentle heat and cook, stirring throughout until the chocolate melts and the icing is smooth and glossy. Remove from the heat and leave to cool for about 20 mins or until the icing has thickened slightly.

Pour over the cake covering it completely and smooth with a palette knife. Make a few swirls if liked around the sides and on the top to give a decorative effect. Leave until set before transferring to a serving plate.

Meanwhile make the chocolate caraque curls. Melt the chocolate in a small bowl over a pan of gently simmering water. Stir until completely smooth then pour on to a marble slab, laminated board or a baking sheet. Using a palette knife spread the chocolate evenly over the surface. Place in the fridge for 10 mins or until firm but not set hard.

Using a large kitchen or palette knife push the blade across the chocolate to form thin scrolls. (If using a laminated board or baking sheet, place on a damp tea towel.) Use cocktail sticks to pick up the scrolls and place them on top of the cake.

Handy tip

Make extra scrolls and store covered in a dry place and use as decorations for desserts, other cakes and as toppings for ice cream.

4. Using a palette knife smooth the icing over the top and sides of the cake. Make a few swirls to give a decorative finish

5. Melt the chocolate in a small bowl, stir until smooth, pour on to a marble slab. Place in fridge until firm

6. Using a large kitchen or palette knife push the blade across the chocolate to form scrolls

GINGERBREAD HOUSE

Delight the children with this charming cake made from spicy, soft gingerbread, decorated with all sorts of sweets and goodies. It'll make their day.

Calories per portion: 536　　　　　　　　　SERVES 12

1. Measure halfway across the top of shorter side and trim down both sides to form a long triangle

2. Spread some icing around the circles and stick the cellophane over. Cover round the outside of window with sweets

3. Spread two of the larger pieces with icing, arrange chocolate buttons over to form roof tiles, leave space for chimney

FOR THE GINGERBREAD:

12 oz/350 g clear honey
4 oz/100 g caster sugar
4 oz/100 g butter or margarine
1 egg, size 3, beaten
½ tsp each of ground mixed spice, ground cinnamon, ground coriander
1 tsp ground ginger
1 tsp baking powder
1 tsp bicarbonate of soda
1 lb 2 oz/500 g plain flour

FOR THE DECORATION:

2 sweets in cellophane wrappers
12 oz/350 g royal icing
8 oz/225 g chocolate buttons
assorted sweets and cake decorations
1 chocolate wafer biscuit
icing sugar to dust

Preheat oven to Gas 4, 350°F, 180°C, 10 mins before baking. Lightly grease and flour three 13 in x 9 in/33 cm x 23 cm baking tins.

Place honey, sugar and fat in a pan and melt slowly – do not boil. Stir in egg, all spices, baking powder and bicarbonate of soda, and mix well. Sieve in the flour and mix to form a smooth dough. Cover and leave for 2-3 hrs. Divide dough into three and roll each portion out on a lightly floured surface to fit each tin. Bake for 20-25 mins until risen and golden. Cool slightly before turning on to wire racks.

Whilst still warm, trim the crusts from the edges of the gingerbread and discard. Cut the gingerbread, using a sharp knife and ruler, into pieces as follows: three pieces: 10 in x 7 in/ 25.5 cm x 18 cm, and three pieces : 6½ in x 5 in/16.5 cm x 12.5 cm.

Taking two of the smaller pieces, measure halfway across the top of shorter side and trim down both sides to form a long triangle. Repeat with other piece. Using a small round cutter stamp out a circle from each piece to form a window, and a small rectangle from one side to form a door. Using the cellophane wrapping from 2 boiled sweets, trim them down to fit the circles, with a bit over. Spread some icing around the insides of the circles and stick the cellophane over. Cover round the outside of the window with sweets and decorations as liked. Set aside to dry.

Spread two of the larger pieces with icing and arrange chocolate buttons over to form roof tiles, leaving a small square on one piece to attach the chimney. Leave to dry for 30 mins.

Place remaining small piece on a cake board or serving plate and spread icing on each narrow end. Stand the two triangle pieces on the base at either end and secure in place using cocktail sticks. Leave to dry for 30 mins.

Spread icing all around the inside edge of the roof portions and gently press on to the triangular end pieces and the base. Carefully trim any pieces that overhang and tile up the middle of the roof section with more chocolate buttons and icing.

Trim the chocolate wafer at an angle so it will sit straight on the roof and secure in position with icing. Leave to set for 30 mins.

With remaining piece of gingerbread stamp out figures and Christmas trees to stand on board. Decorate as desired.

Spread icing over roof top and chimney to resemble snow and attach a small piece of cotton wool to the chimney to resemble smoke. Attach figures and tree to the board and the door to the door frame using icing, and dust with icing sugar to serve.

HANDY TIP

This is best eaten within two days. To store longer, wrap closely with tin foil, taking care not to damage the decoration and keep in a cool, dry place for up to one week.

4. Stand the two triangle pieces on the base at either end and secure in place using cocktail sticks

5. Carefully trim any pieces that overhang, tile the middle section of the roof with more chocolate buttons and icing

6. Trim the chocolate wafer at an angle and secure on the roof with icing. Leave to set for 30 mins

Panettone

For something a little different, try a taste of Italy with this light and airy traditional Italian Christmas bread filled with candied peel, sultanas and raisins. A real treat any time of year.

Calories per portion: 409

Makes 1 x 2 lb/900 g loaf

14 oz/400 g strong plain flour
1 oz/25 g fresh yeast
1 tsp caster sugar
¼ pint/150 ml milk, warmed
1 egg, size 3
2 egg yolks, size 3
3 tbsp vanilla sugar
1 tsp salt
4½ oz/120 g butter
3 oz/75 g candied citron peel, finely chopped
2 oz/50 g golden sultanas
2 oz/50 g raisins
2 tsp icing sugar, sifted
candied citron peel to decorate

Preheat oven to Gas 6, 400°F, 200°C, 15 mins before baking. Grease a 6 in/15 cm round x 3 in/7.5 cm deep cake tin and line with baking parchment. Dust with flour. Tie a foil collar around outside of tin with string, to come 3 in/7.5 cm above rim of tin, and grease and flour.

Sieve flour into large mixing bowl. Cream yeast and caster sugar until smooth and blend with 2 tbsp of milk and 2 tbsp of flour to form a batter. Cover with greased clearwrap, leave in warm place for 30 mins or until spongy.

Mix together egg, egg yolks, vanilla sugar and salt. Melt 4 oz/100 g butter and add to egg mixture along with yeast 'sponge'. Make a well in centre of flour, add egg, yeast mixture and remaining milk and mix to form a smooth, elastic dough. Turn on to a lightly floured surface and knead until smooth. Place dough in a clean, greased mixing bowl. Cover with greased clearwrap and leave in warm place until doubled in size – about 1-2 hrs.

Re-knead the dough until smooth and elastic again. Return to bowl, cover again and leave until doubled in size again. Flatten dough out slightly and sprinkle with peel, sultanas and raisins. Fold dough over and knead to incorporate fruit. Form into a ball and place in centre of tin.

Using a sharp knife, cut a 3½ in/9 cm cross on top. Cover loosely with greased clearwrap, place in warm place until domed part of dough has risen to top of foil. Uncover, re-cut cross and place remaining butter in centre of cross. Bake for 10 mins, then lower oven to Gas 4, 350°F, 180°C. Bake for a further 45-50 mins or until a skewer inserted into centre comes out clean.

Leave to cool in tin for 15 mins, then remove foil. Place tin on side and gently remove loaf. Stand on wire rack to cool completely. Sprinkle with icing sugar.

Handy tip

If preferred, make in advance and freeze until required. When ready to eat the bread, warm through gently then slice and serve immediately.

1. Tie foil around the outside of tin with string – to come 3 in/7.5 cm above rim

2. Sieve flour into bowl, cream yeast and sugar, blend with milk and flour

3. Make a well in centre of flour, add egg and yeast mixture and remaining milk

4. Flatten dough out slightly, sprinkle with dried fruit. Fold dough over and knead

5. When risen, uncover dough, re-cut and place remaining butter in centre of cross

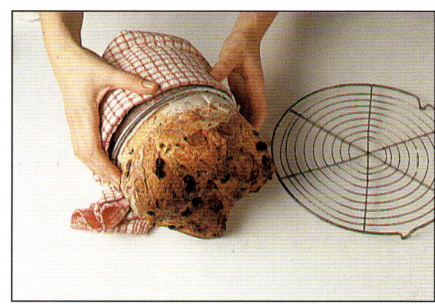

6. After baking, cool. Place tin on side and gently remove loaf. Transfer to wire rack

Strawberry Tarts

Crisp, melt-in-the-mouth pastry, filled with smooth chocolate and velvety-rich custard, topped with luscious strawberries, make these delicious tarts a really wicked treat for the whole family to enjoy!

Calories per portion: 393

Makes 6

FOR THE PASTRY:
6 oz/175 g plain white flour
4 oz/100 g butter or margarine
1 egg yolk, size 5

FOR THE FILLING:
½ pint/300 ml semi-skimmed milk
1 tbsp plain white flour
1 egg, size 5
1 tbsp caster sugar
1 tsp butter
2-3 drops vanilla essence
3 oz/75 g plain chocolate

FOR THE TOPPING:
8 oz/225 g strawberries, hulled, washed and lightly dried
3 tbsp redcurrant jelly
1 tbsp lemon juice

Preheat the oven to Gas 6, 400°F, 200°C, 15 mins before baking the pastry cases.

Sieve the flour into a bowl. Cut the fat into cubes and add to the flour with the egg yolk and 1 tsp cold water. Using your hands, work the mixture together to form a pliable, but not sticky, dough. Wrap, then chill for at least 1 hr. Roll the dough out on a lightly floured surface. Use to line six 3 in/7.5 cm individual fluted flan or patty tins.

Prick the bases lightly with a fork, then place a small sheet of greaseproof paper and some baking beans in each one. Bake blind for 12-15 mins, or until the pastry is cooked. Remove from the oven, discard the paper and baking beans and leave until cold.

To make the filling, warm the milk to blood heat. Place the flour in a small bowl, add the egg, then beat until smooth. Gradually beat the warmed milk into the flour and egg mixture, then strain into a clean pan. Return to heat and cook gently, stirring throughout, until mixture thickens and coats the back of a wooden spoon. Remove from the heat and beat in the sugar, butter and vanilla essence. Pour the custard into a small bowl, then cover with damp greaseproof paper and leave to one side until cold.

When the pastry cases are cold, melt the plain chocolate in a small bowl, over a pan of simmering water. Carefully brush insides of cases with chocolate, then leave until the chocolate has set. Beat the cooled custard to ensure there are no lumps, then spoon into pastry cases. Arrange strawberries attractively over the custard filling.

Heat the redcurrant jelly and lemon juice together and stir until smooth. Leave to cool slightly, then use to coat the strawberries. Leave for at least 15 mins to allow the glaze to set before serving.

Handy Tip

Replace the strawberries with any prepared ripe soft fruit – alternatively use well-drained canned fruit such as apricots, then use apricot jam and lemon juice for glazing.

1. Line tins with pastry. Prick bases, place greaseproof and baking beans in each tin

2. Heat milk, beat into flour and egg. Strain into clean pan, cook until thickened

3. Once the pastry cases have cooled, brush the insides with melted chocolate

CAKES & BAKES 47

4. Leave the chocolate to set, then fill the tarts with the cooled, prepared custard

5. Arrange the washed and hulled strawberries attractively over the custard

6. Allow redcurrant jelly and lemon juice to cool slightly, brush over strawberries

Eccles Cakes

Delicious rounds of feather-light flaky pastry, filled with a lightly spiced currant mixture, these classic cakes from Lancashire just melt in the mouth! Serve them warm for a super-tasty mid-morning snack or as a winning tea-time treat.

Calories per portion: 303 | Makes 8 cakes

1. Rub one quarter of fat into flour. Mix to a dough with water and lemon juice

2. Roll chilled dough into an oblong. Dot a quarter of the fat over top two thirds

3. Fold bottom third of pastry up over centre third. Cover this with top third

Cakes & Bakes

- 8 oz/225 g plain flour
- 8 oz/225 g self-raising wholemeal flour
- 1½ tsp mixed spice
- 3 tsp ground ginger
- 3 oz/75 g demerara sugar
- 3 oz/75 g sultanas
- 3 oz/75 g mixed peel
- 8 oz/225 g butter or margarine
- 8 oz/225 g golden syrup
- 8 oz/225 g black treacle
- 2 eggs, size 3, beaten
- 1 pint/600 ml milk
- 2 tsp bicarbonate of soda

FOR THE GLACÉ ICING:
- 12 oz/350 g icing sugar
- juice 2 large lemons, strained
- stem ginger to decorate

Preheat oven to Gas 4, 350°F, 180°C, 10 mins before baking. Grease and line base of a 10 in x 8 in/26 cm x 20.5 cm oblong cake tin with greased greaseproof paper.

Place flours and spices in a large bowl and mix together. Stir in sugar, sultanas and mixed peel. Place fat, syrup and black treacle in a bowl and heat over a pan of gently simmering water until melted. Stir occasionally, then beat into the flour and fruit. Then gradually beat in the eggs, ensuring they are thoroughly blended in.

Heat the milk to blood heat, then add the bicarbonate of soda and stir until dissolved. Beat milk into the mixture to form a smooth batter with no lumps. Pour into prepared tin.

Bake on centre shelf for 50-60 mins, or until cooked. To test if cooked, insert a skewer into the centre and if it comes out clean, the gingerbread is cooked. Remove from oven and leave to cool for 5 mins, then turn out on to a wire cooling rack and discard lining paper. Leave until cold before coating with icing.

Sieve icing sugar into a mixing bowl, then gradually beat in the lemon juice and sufficient hot water to make a smooth icing. It should be thick enough to coat the back of a wooden spoon. Pour over top of gingerbread and spread evenly with a palette knife.

Decorate with small pieces of stem ginger. Cut into squares when cold.

HANDY TIP

Keep the gingerbread in an airtight tin, not a plastic container.

1. Add the mixed peel and sultanas to the flour, spices and demerara sugar

2. Melt the fat, syrup and treacle in a bowl over a pan of simmering water

3. Beat melted ingredients into flour, fruit and spices, mixing together well

4. Add beaten eggs to gingerbread mixture. Beat until completely blended in

5. Pour mixture into a greased and lined tin, allow mixture to find its own level

6. Pour icing on to cooled gingerbread and spread over top with a palette knife

Doughnuts

You'll be in everyone's good books if you make these delicious doughnuts! Try them ring or jam-filled and tossed in lemon-flavoured caster sugar. Serve them while they're still warm.

Calories per portion: 217 **Makes 9**

- 8 oz/225 g strong plain white flour
- ½ tsp salt
- 1 x 6 g sachet easy-blend yeast
- 4 oz/100 g caster sugar
- 1 oz/25 g butter
- 3-4 fl oz/75-120 ml milk
- 1 egg, size 3, beaten
- 1½ tbsp seedless raspberry jam
- oil for deep-fat frying
- grated rind 1 lemon

Sift flour and salt into a large mixing bowl and stir in easy-blend yeast and ½ oz/15 g of the caster sugar. Cut butter into small pieces then rub into the flour until mixture resembles fine breadcrumbs. Then warm the milk to blood heat. Make a well in the centre of dry ingredients and stir in beaten egg. Mix to a smooth, not sticky, dough with the warmed milk. Knead on a lightly floured surface until smooth and pliable.

Lightly grease the cleaned mixing bowl with a little oil then return the dough to the bowl and cover, either with a clean tea towel or clearwrap, or place inside a large polythene bag. Leave in a warm place away from draughts or direct heat for 1-2 hrs or until doubled in size.

Turn out on to a lightly floured surface and knead again until smooth. Divide dough in half, roll out one half and cut into 3 in/7.5 cm rounds. Cut out centres using a 1 in/2.5 cm plain cutter. Put the trimmings together and roll out again until all the dough has been used.

Cut the remaining dough into 4-5 balls and pat or roll them into 3 in/7.5 cm rounds. Place 1 tsp raspberry jam in the centre then form into a ball and pinch together firmly to encase the jam. Place on a lightly greased baking sheet. Cover with a piece of muslin or lightly oiled clearwrap and leave the doughnuts in a warm place until doubled in size – about 30-45 mins.

Bring the oil in a deep-fat fryer to 375°F, 190°C. If you don't have a thermometer, the oil has reached the correct temperature when a cube of bread turns golden after 30 seconds. Fry the doughnuts a few at a time for 2-3 mins on each side. Turn with a spatula to cook the other side.

Mix the remaining sugar with the lemon rind, place either on a sheet of greaseproof paper or in a polythene bag. When the doughnuts are golden brown and cooked through, drain well on absorbent kitchen paper, then toss in the sugar and lemon rind until thoroughly coated. The doughnuts are best eaten while still warm.

Handy tip

Vary the flavour by adding grated lemon rind or ground cinnamon to the basic mixture.

1. Sift the flour and salt into a large mixing bowl, then rub in the butter

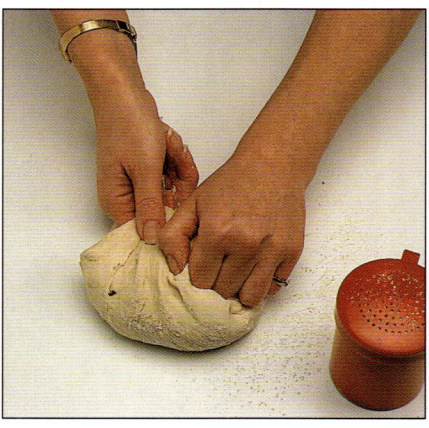

2. Using the knuckles, knead the dough well until it is smooth and pliable

3. After proving, the dough should have doubled in size. Knead again until smooth

CAKES & BAKES

4. Use one half of dough for ring doughnuts and other half for jam ones

5. Roll or pat dough to a 3 in/7.5 cm round, place a spoonful of jam in centre

6. Fry a few of the doughnuts at a time in hot oil for 2-3 mins on each side

Chelsea Buns

Bake the best-ever Chelsea Buns! Filled with plump raisins, sultanas and currants, and just a hint of cinnamon, they're delicious, especially when eaten warm. Follow this easy step-by-step recipe and give the family a tasty tea-time treat.

Calories per portion: 491   Makes 12

Cakes & Bakes

- 1 lb/450 g strong white plain flour
- ½ level tsp salt
- 3 tsp dried yeast
- 8 fl oz/250 ml milk, tepid
- 2 tsp caster sugar
- 3 oz/75 g butter
- 1 egg, size 1, beaten
- 8 oz/225 g mixed dried fruit
- 4 oz/100 g light soft brown sugar
- 2 tsp ground cinnamon
- 1-2 tbsp clear honey

Preheat oven to Gas 5, 375°F, 190°C, 10 mins before baking. Lightly grease a 12 in x 10 in/30 cm x 25 cm baking tin. Sieve the flour and salt into a mixing bowl. Sprinkle yeast over ¼ pint/150 ml milk, add a pinch of caster sugar, stir. Leave for 15 mins or until frothy.

Meanwhile cut the butter into small cubes, then rub into the flour until the mixture resembles fine breadcrumbs. Make a well in the centre, then pour in the yeast and milk mixture, remaining milk and beaten egg. Bring ingredients together to form a soft, but not sticky, dough, which doesn't cling to the bowl. Turn on to a lightly floured surface and knead until smooth and elastic. Place in a lightly oiled bowl, cover with oiled clearwrap or a clean tea towel and prove in a warm place for 1 hr or until doubled in size.

Turn out dough on to a lightly floured surface, knead again then roll out to a 12 in x 9 in/30 cm x 22.5 cm oblong. Mix together the dried fruit, sugar and cinnamon and spoon over the dough to within ½ in/1.25 cm of the edge. Roll up the dough tightly lengthways, as you would for a Swiss roll. Press edges together firmly to seal. Cut the roll into 1½ in/4 cm rounds. Lay each round flat in greased baking tin. Cover with oiled clearwrap or a clean tea towel and leave for 30 mins or until doubled in size.

Bake in oven for 30 mins or until well risen. Warm honey then brush over cooked buns, sprinkle with remaining caster sugar. Cool slightly before turning out.

Handy tips

Add 1 tsp ground cinnamon to the basic dough and sprinkle the cooked buns with demerara sugar for a crunchy topping.

1. Sieve flour into mixing bowl. Sprinkle dried yeast over ¼ pint/150 ml milk

2. Bring all the ingredients together to form a soft, but not sticky, dough

3. Knead the dough on a lightly floured surface until smooth and elastic

4. Roll out to a 12 in x 9 in/30 cm x 22.5 cm oblong. Spoon over dry ingredients

5. Roll up the dough tightly lengthways, as you would for a Swiss roll

6. Cut dough into 1½ in/4 cm rounds, place close together in a greased tin

CRUMPETS

Cook a tasty tea-time treat and serve these delicious wholemeal crumpets. Toasted and then spread lightly with butter, you'll enjoy every golden mouthful. They're very easy to make and so much nicer than the shop bought ones.

Calories per portion: 118 — **Makes 10**

- 6 oz/175 g plain flour
- 2oz/50 g wholemeal flour
- ½ tsp salt
- ½ oz/15 g fresh yeast or 1½ tsp dried yeast, or 1 x 6 g sachet easy-blend dried yeast
- 2 tsp clear honey
- 12 fl oz/350 ml milk, warmed
- 1-2 tbsp vegetable oil

Sift flours and salt into a large bowl and leave in a warm place while creaming fresh yeast. Blend yeast with the honey then pour on the warmed milk. Stir and leave in a warm place for approx 15 mins or until liquid is frothy.

If using dried yeast, dissolve honey in the warmed milk, sprinkle the dried yeast on top, stir lightly, then leave in a warm place away from any draughts for 10-15 mins until frothy.

Pour frothy liquid into warmed flour in a steady stream, beating as you go to form a smooth batter. Beat well then cover with either clearwrap or a clean tea towel. Leave in a warm place away from draughts for 40-50 mins until batter is frothy.

If making crumpets with easy-blend dried yeast, place flours and salt in bowl and leave in a warm place for 15 mins. Dissolve honey in milk, then stir into flours and add yeast, mix to a batter, then cover and leave for 45 mins or until frothy. Before cooking the crumpets, transfer the batter to a measuring jug for easy pouring.

Lightly grease a heavy-based frying pan or griddle and either some crumpet rings or 4 in/10 cm plain cutters with the oil. When hot pour in ½ in/1.25 cm of the batter into each ring and cook over a moderate heat for 5-8 mins or until bubbles burst. Remove rings, turn crumpets and cook for 1 min.

The crumpets can now be removed from the pan, stored in an airtight tin and toasted later the same day. Otherwise remove rings or cutters and turn crumpets over and cook on the other side for 1 min. Drain on absorbent kitchen paper and serve immediately spread with butter.

Handy tips

If you prefer white crumpets simply replace the wholemeal flour with plain white flour and proceed with the recipe. The crumpets are best eaten on the same day or may be frozen and used within two months.

1. Cream yeast with honey until smooth, beat in warm milk, leave until frothy

2. Add the frothy yeast and milk mixture to the flours then beat in well

3. Beat to a smooth batter ensuring there are no lumps left in the mixture

CAKES & BAKES

4. Cover batter with clearwrap and leave in a warm place for 40-50 mins

5. Grease frying pan or griddle and crumpet rings, then pour in batter

6. When bubbles have burst, remove rings, turn crumpets and cook for 1 min

Mince Pies

Christmas just wouldn't be the same without mince pies! So why not give everyone a real treat by making your own mincemeat with this deliciously rich but healthy recipe, which is also suitable for vegetarians.

Calories per 1 lb/450 g: 1,225; per 1 oz/25 g: 77   **Makes 7 lb/3 kg**

1 lb/450 g carrots
8 oz/225 g parsnips
1 lb/450 g cooking apples
1 lb/450 g currants
1 lb/450 g sultanas
1 lb/450 g seedless raisins
4 oz/100 g mixed chopped peel
4 oz/100 g whole almonds, blanched
1 lb/450 g muscovado sugar
8 oz/225 g vegetable suet
1 tsp grated nutmeg
1 tsp ground cinnamon
½ tsp ground mace
½ tsp ground cloves
2 lemons
1 large or 2 small oranges
4-6 tbsp brandy

FOR 18 MINCE PIES:
1 lb/450 g prepared shortcrust pastry
8 oz/225 g prepared mincemeat

Preheat oven to Gas 6, 400°F, 200°C, 15 mins before baking pies. Peel carrots, parsnips and cooking apples. Discard apple core. Grate carrots, parsnips and apples coarsely and place in a large mixing bowl. Stir in the currants, sultanas, raisins and mixed peel. Chop almonds fairly small and add to mixture with the sugar, suet and spices. Stir well.

Scrub the lemons and orange well and dry thoroughly. Then grate the rind finely and squeeze out the juice. Add to the mixture with sufficient brandy to give a moist consistency. The exact amount of brandy will vary slightly as this will depend on the amount of juice obtained from the lemons and orange.

Stir well, then pot in clean dry jars, packing the mixture down with the back of a spoon. Cover with a waxed disc and cellophane covers. Label clearly. Leave in a cool dry place for two weeks to mature.

When ready, make your mince pies. Roll out the pastry on a lightly floured surface and cut into 18 x 3 in/7.5 cm rounds with a fluted pastry cutter. Use to line 18 bun or patty tins. Roll out the remaining pastry and cut out the same number of 2½ in/6.5 cm fluted rounds and reserve for lids.

Place a heaped tsp of mature mincemeat in the centre of each of the pastry-lined tins. Dampen edges with a little water then place lids in position and press edges together. Brush tops with a little water and sprinkle them with a little caster sugar. Make a small slit in the centre of each mince pie to allow steam to escape. Bake for 15-20 mins or until cooked.

Dredge with a little extra sugar before serving. This mincemeat should be used within eight weeks of maturing.

Handy tip

To press edges of pies together, turn an egg cup upside down, dust the opening with flour then place on top of mince pies and press down lightly.

1. Prepare ingredients before. Weigh fruit and grate parsnips, carrot and apple

2. Mix all the ingredients in a large mixing bowl, stirring with a wooden spoon

3. Finely grate nutmeg into mixture. Add remaining spices, rind and juice of fruit

CAKES & BAKES 59

4. Pack mincemeat into 1 lb/450 g jars. Press down with back of a spoon

5. When ready to use, line tins with pastry and place 1 heaped tsp in centre

6. Dampen edges of pastry and place lids in position. Press edges together

Danish Pastries

Flaky golden pastries, filled with a selection of scrumptious fillings and glazed with apricot jam, make a delicious treat for any time of the day. Crescents, Windmills, Cockscombs, Pinwheels... every shape is so simple to make.

Calories per portion: 235   **Makes 28**

1. Rub fat into flour, stir in sugar, beat egg into milk, add to flour with yeast

2. Roll out dough, place rolled butter on top. Fold pastry to encase butter

3. Roll dough into two strips, place marzipan in centre, fold, seal, cut out combs

FOR THE DOUGH:
- 1 lb/450 g plain white flour
- 2 oz/50 g lard or white vegetable fat
- 2 level tbsp sugar
- 2 eggs, size 3
- 7 fl oz/200 ml milk, warmed
- ½ oz/15 g easy-blend dried yeast
- 8 oz/225 g butter

FOR THE COCKSCOMBS:
- 6 oz/175 g white marzipan

FOR THE WINDMILLS:
- 4 canned apricot halves, drained
- ½ oz/15 g flaked almonds

FOR THE PINWHEELS:
- 4 oz/100 g mixed dried fruit
- 2 oz/50 g soft brown sugar
- 1 tsp ground mixed spice

FOR THE CRESCENTS:
- 2 oz/50 g butter
- 2 oz/50 g soft brown sugar
- ½ tsp ground cinnamon

FOR THE GLAZE AND DECORATION:
- 6 tbsp apricot jam
- juice of ½ lemon, strained
- 2 oz/50 g icing sugar, sieved

Preheat the oven to Gas 7, 425°F, 220°C, 15 mins before baking the pastries. Sieve flour into a bowl, rub in fat until mixture resembles breadcrumbs. Add sugar. Beat 1 egg into milk, then add to flour mixture with yeast and mix to a soft pliable dough. Knead for 5 mins or until dough is shiny and smooth. Wrap and allow to rest for 10 mins.

Place butter between two sheets of greaseproof and roll out to an oblong. On a lightly floured surface, roll pastry out to an oblong three times longer than the butter. Place butter in centre of dough, fold over and seal, encasing the butter completely. Wrap and chill for 10 mins. Repeat rolling and folding twice more. Divide pastry in four.

To make the Cockscombs, roll pastry into two long strips, approx 4 in × 12 in/10 cm × 30 cm each. Divide the marzipan in half and shape each piece into a long thin roll. Place the marzipan rolls in centre of pastry strips, brush pastry edges with the remaining egg, beaten, and fold the pastry over, sealing the edges well. Cut into 3 in/7.5 cm lengths, then make 3-4 small cuts in pastry edges, towards marzipan. Bend slightly into a curve.

For the Windmills, roll pastry out and cut into four 4 in/10 cm squares. Place 1 apricot in centre of each. Cut the four corners towards the centre, then bring corners into centre to form a windmill. Secure pastry with the beaten egg, then brush all over with egg and sprinkle with the flaked almonds.

For Pinwheels, roll pastry out to an oblong, 12 in × 8 in/30 cm × 20.5 cm. Sprinkle with the fruit, sugar and mixed spice, brush the edges with beaten egg and roll up. Cut into eight 1 in/2.5 cm pieces. Place on baking sheet.

For the Crescents, roll pastry into two 8 in/20.5 cm circles and cut each into quarters. Cream butter, sugar and cinnamon together, then place at pointed end of each quarter. Brush with egg, roll up and bend to form a crescent. Seal edges.

Leave pastries on a greased baking sheet to prove for 20 mins, brush again with egg, then bake for 12-15 mins.

Meanwhile, heat jam and lemon juice. Sieve. When pastries are cooked, brush with glaze. When cold, mix icing sugar with 1 tsp hot water. Place in a piping bag with a plain icing nozzle, pipe thin lines across or over the Pinwheels and Crescents to decorate.

HANDY TIP

Once cold, freeze. When required, thaw, then warm through before serving.

4. Cut dough into squares, place an apricot in the centre, cut corners and fold

5. Roll dough out to a rectangle, sprinkle with fruit, sugar and spice, roll up and cut

6. Roll dough into two circles, quarter. Roll up into crescents, encasing filling

Tea Cakes

Originating from Yorkshire, these fruity buns are just the thing for a tea-time treat. They're simply delicious served warm with butter – or, for an extra indulgence, split them in half, lightly toast then spread with butter and strawberry jam.

Calories per portion: 340 **Serves 8**

- 1 lb/450 g strong plain white flour
- pinch of salt
- 2 oz/50 g butter or margarine
- 2 tsp easy-blend dried yeast
- 1 oz/25 g caster sugar
- 2 oz/50 g chopped mixed peel
- 4 oz/100 g currants
- ½ pint/300 ml semi-skimmed milk
- 1 tbsp milk to glaze

Preheat the oven to Gas 6, 400°F, 200°C, 15 mins before baking tea cakes. Lightly oil two baking sheets. Sieve the flour and pinch of salt into a large mixing bowl, then add the butter or margarine and rub into the flour until mixture resembles fine breadcrumbs. Sprinkle in the easy-blend dried yeast, then add the caster sugar, chopped mixed peel and currants.

Warm the semi-skimmed milk, pour into the mixing bowl and mix to a soft, but not sticky, dough. Turn out on to a lightly floured surface and knead for about 5-10 mins, or until smooth. Transfer the dough to a clean, lightly oiled bowl, cover, then leave in a warm place for 1 hr, or until doubled in size. (Do not leave the dough in a draught, or it won't rise.)

When the dough has risen, turn out on a lightly floured surface. Using your knuckles, knock the dough down, then, using one hand, pull the dough out (taking care not to tear it), then push it back to the centre, kneading until smooth and elastic. (The more you knead the dough, the lighter your tea cakes will be.)

Shape the dough into a 16 in/41 cm long roll, then carefully cut into eight equal-sized pieces. Using your hands, lightly dusted with flour, revolve each piece between your hands to form a perfect round. Place four rounds on to each oiled baking sheet, then flatten lightly with the palm of your hand. Cover, then leave again in a warm place for 20-30 mins, or until doubled in size. (The dough should spring back when lightly touched with a clean finger.)

Brush the tops of the tea cakes with a little milk, then bake in the oven for 20 mins, or until golden brown and cooked. To test if the tea cakes are cooked, lightly tap the base of each – it should sound hollow. Leave the tea cakes to cool on a wire rack.

To serve, split the cooled tea cakes in half, toast lightly, then spread them with butter. Serve with home-made strawberry jam. The tea cakes are best eaten the same day.

Handy tip

For a change, add to the sieved flour, either 1 tsp ground cinnamon, 1 tsp mixed spice, or the grated rind of 1 lemon.

1. Sieve flour and salt into a large mixing bowl, then add fat and rub into flour. Sprinkle in yeast

2. Add the caster sugar, chopped mixed peel and currants to the mixture in the bowl

3. Warm the milk, then pour into the mixing bowl and mix to a soft, but not sticky, dough

CAKES & BAKES 63

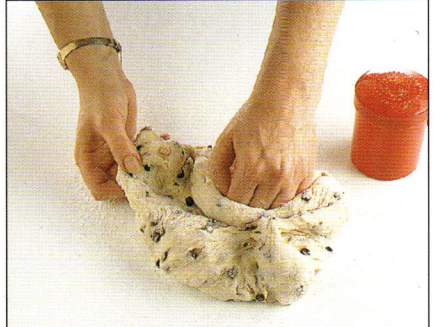

4. Turn the dough out on a lightly floured surface. Using your knuckles, knead well until the dough is smooth and elastic

5. Shape the dough into a 16 in/41 cm long roll, then carefully cut into eight equal-sized portions

6. Lightly dust hands with flour, shape dough into rounds, then place on baking sheets

Chocolate Brownies

The secret of this American classic is the pecan nut taste. Add to that a truly delicious chocolate sponge and a dreamy fudge-icing topping and you have a taste of heaven that the family will love!

Calories per portion: 351 **Cuts into 20**

- 8 oz/225 g butter or margarine
- 4 oz/100 g plain chocolate
- 14 oz/400 g granulated sugar
- 4 eggs, size 3
- 6 oz/175 g plain flour
- 1 tsp vanilla essence
- ½ tsp salt
- 3 oz/75 g milk chocolate
- 3 oz/75 g pecan nuts

FOR THE TOPPING:
- 2 oz/50 g plain chocolate
- 1 oz/25 g butter or margarine
- 3½ oz/90 g icing sugar
- 2-3 tbsp milk
- 2 oz/50 g white chocolate

Preheat the oven to Gas 4, 350°F, 180°C, 10 mins before baking. Grease and base-line a 13 in x 9 in/33 cm x 23 cm baking tin with a piece of lightly oiled grease-proof paper.

Place fat in a heatproof bowl. Break plain chocolate into pieces, add to bowl and place over a pan of gently simmering water.

Heat gently, stirring occasionally until melted. Remove the bowl from the pan and stir in the granulated sugar. Allow the mixture to cool for 10 mins and then add the eggs, one at a time and whisk in, ensuring they are thoroughly incorporated.

Sieve flour into the mixture and fold in using a metal spoon. Add the vanilla essence and salt. Chop milk chocolate into small pieces and roughly chop pecans. Add chocolate and nuts to cake mixture, then stir thoroughly. Spoon into prepared tin, smooth top and bake for 40 mins, or until cooked.

To test if the cake is cooked, insert a clean skewer into the centre – it should come out clean. Place tin on a wire rack and allow the cake to cool completely before making topping.

To make topping, melt the plain chocolate and fat in a bowl over a pan of gently simmering water, stirring occasionally. Remove the bowl from the heat, then sieve in the icing sugar and whisk until smooth. Add sufficient milk to give a spreading consistency, and then spread over the top of the cake. Leave to set for 30 mins. Cut into 20 portions, then transfer brownies individually to a wire rack.

Melt the white chocolate in a bowl over a pan of gently simmering water and stir until smooth. Remove from the heat, then, using a small spoon or fork, drizzle the white chocolate over the brownies. Leave them to set completely before serving.

Handy tip

Substitute 3 oz/75 g chopped almonds for the pecan nuts and add 3 oz/75 g chopped dates to the basic mixture.

1. Melt plain chocolate and fat over hot water, remove from heat and stir in sugar

2. When the chocolate mixture has cooled slightly, whisk in the eggs, one at a time

3. Sieve flour into mixture and fold in. Add vanilla essence, salt, chocolate and nuts

CAKES & BAKES

4. To ensure that the cake is thoroughly cooked, insert a clean skewer into centre

5. For the topping, melt the chocolate and fat together, then whisk in the icing sugar

6. Decorate the iced brownies by drizzling the melted white chocolate over the top

STRAWBERRY SHORTCAKES

Just perfect for a summer tea-time treat, deliciously crisp, shortcake biscuits, topped with whipped cream and luscious ripe strawberries, these strawberry shortcakes are a must for everyone.

Calories per biscuit: 319　　　　**Makes 10**

- 8 oz/225 g plain flour
- 6 oz/175 g butter or margarine
- 3 oz/75 g caster sugar
- ½ pint/300 ml whipping cream
- 8 oz/225 g strawberries, hulled

Preheat oven to Gas 4, 350°F, 180°C, 10 mins before baking. Lightly grease two baking sheets. Sieve the flour into a large mixing bowl. Add the butter or margarine together with the sugar. With cool hands and keeping the fat in one piece, gradually work in the flour and sugar until mixture forms a ball in the centre of the bowl and the sides are clean.

Knead on a lightly floured surface until smooth and free from cracks. Roll out to ¼ in/6 mm thick then cut into 20 x 2½ in/6.5 cm rounds with a fluted pastry cutter. Take care not to use too much flour when rolling out as this will alter the texture of the biscuits. Place on the baking sheets ensuring that they are spaced slightly apart to allow for spreading.

Prick lightly with a fork then bake for 15-25 mins or until lightly golden brown. Allow to cool for 1 min then transfer to wire cooling racks until the biscuits are completely cold.

Whip the cream until stiff and standing in soft peaks. Spoon into a piping bag fitted with a large fluted nozzle. Pipe the cream on to half the biscuits, covering the biscuit completely. Pipe a rosette in the centre of the remaining biscuits. If the strawberries are large, cut them in half or slice, then arrange on top of the cream-covered biscuits as shown. Place a whole strawberry in the centre of the rosette of cream. Sandwich biscuits together and eat on the same day.

HANDY TIPS

The plain biscuits can be stored for up to one week in an airtight tin. If you would like a slightly healthier version of the shortbread – try using 3 oz/75 g wholemeal flour, 5 oz/150 g white flour, 6 oz/175 g polyunsaturated margarine, 2 oz/50 g soft brown sugar. Proceed as instructed for the biscuits. Whip ¼ pint/150 ml whipping cream and fold in ¼ pint/150 ml fromage frais or low-fat natural yogurt. Alternatively, make the shortbread as directed, then roll out on a lightly floured surface. Cut into two 7 in/18 cm rounds, ¼ in/6 mm thick. Prick lightly with a fork and then cook at Gas 8, 450°F, 230°C for 12-15 mins or until the biscuits are pale golden in colour. Remove from the oven and allow to cool for 1 min. Carefully transfer to wire cooling racks. Leave until completely cold, then fill as for little shortcakes. Eat as soon as possible!

1. Have the fat at room temperature before adding it to the flour

2. Keep hands cool while working the fat into the dry ingredients

3. Work the fat into the flour and sugar until mixture forms a ball

CAKES & BAKES 67

4. Dust the surface and the rolling pin lightly with flour when rolling out

5. Use a palette knife to lift the rounds of shortbread on to cooling rack

6. Place the tip of the strawberries towards the edge of the biscuits

CROISSANTS

France is famous for its cuisine and one of the best things to come across the channel must be their croissants. Delicious flakes of buttery pastry that just melt in the mouth as you eat them.

Calories per portion: 233 **Makes 16**

1 lb/450 g strong white flour
pinch of salt
1 oz/25 g sugar
1 oz/25 g milk powder
1 oz/25 g lard
1 x 6 g sachet easy-blend yeast
1 egg, size 3
8 oz/225 g unsalted butter
beaten egg to glaze

Preheat oven to Gas 7, 425°F, 220°C, 15 mins before baking the croissants.

Sift the flour into the bowl and stir in the salt, sugar and milk powder. Cut the lard into small pieces then rub into the flour until the mixture resembles fine breadcrumbs. Sprinkle in the easy-blend yeast then mix to a soft and pliable dough with the egg and approx 8 fl oz/250 ml of tepid water.

Turn out on a lightly floured surface and knead until the dough is smooth and free from cracks. Place in a clean and lightly oiled bowl, cover and leave in a warm place for approx 30 mins or until doubled in size. Turn out on to a lightly floured surface and knock the dough down. Knead very lightly then return to the bowl, cover and leave to relax in the fridge for 1 hr.

Roll the dough out to an oblong 20 in x 8 in/51 cm x 20.5 cm and divide the butter into three. Dot the top with two thirds of the dough with small pats of butter then fold the bottom portion up to the centre and the top third down to the centre. Gently seal the edges with the rolling pin then half turn the dough so that the seal is on the side. Wrap in greaseproof and chill in the fridge for 30 mins.

Repeat the rolling, folding and chilling twice more until the butter is used. Wrap again and chill for a further 30 mins. Roll and fold the dough three more times (this is after you have added all the butter) then leave to rest in the fridge for 1 hr.

Roll the dough out on a lightly floured surface to an oblong 12 in x 24 in/30 cm x 61 cm and trim the edges. Cut the dough lengthways in half then into squares and finally into triangles. Brush the triangles very lightly with the beaten egg then starting from the long end, roll up to form crescents.

Place on baking sheets, cover and leave for 30 mins. Brush with egg, bake for 10-15 mins or until cooked. Serve.

HANDY TIP

After brushing the top of the croissants with the beaten egg, try sprinkling with grated cheese, poppy or sesame seeds.

1. Sift the flour into the bowl, stir in salt, sugar and milk powder. Rub in lard, add the yeast, mix to a soft dough with water

2. Roll the dough out on a lightly floured surface then dot top two thirds of the dough with the butter

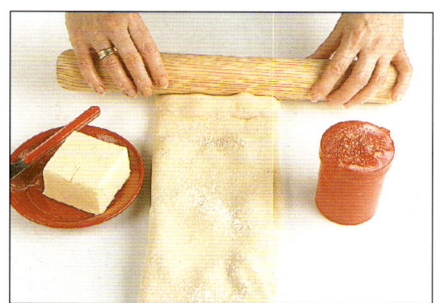

3. Lightly seal the edges of the dough with the rolling pin, half turn dough, wrap and leave to rest in the fridge for 30 mins

4. Roll out the rested dough on a lightly floured surface, to an oblong, trim edges, cut in half then in squares

5. Cut the squares into triangles, brush very lightly with beaten egg, roll up starting from the long end

6. Place the croissants on to a baking sheet, cover and allow to relax for 30 mins. Brush with egg then bake

Herb & Cheese Loaf

Packed full of flavour, this delicious bread with cheeses, herbs and garlic, makes a tasty and satisfying snack or accompaniment. It is best served warm with butter.

Calories per portion: 306 **Serves 8**

¾ oz/20 g fresh yeast
1 tsp caster sugar
¼ pint/150 ml milk
1 lb/450 g wholemeal flour
4 tbsp freshly grated Parmesan cheese
6 oz/175 g Cheddar cheese, grated
1 garlic clove, peeled and crushed
1 tbsp each of freshly chopped basil, parsley and thyme
1 tsp salt
freshly ground black pepper
1 egg, size 5, beaten
1 tbsp poppy seeds
1 tbsp sesame seeds

Preheat oven to Gas 7, 425°F, 220°C, 15 mins before baking bread. Grease and line an 8 in/20.5 cm round cake tin. Place the yeast in a small bowl or jug with the sugar and cream together until smooth. Heat the milk to blood heat and gradually add to the yeast, mixing well, leave to one side until frothy (this will take approx 10-15 mins).

Place the flour in a bowl and mix in the Parmesan cheese, 4 oz/100 g of the Cheddar cheese, the crushed garlic, the herbs and seasoning. Stir in the frothy yeast mixture and approx ¼ pint/150 ml tepid water and mix together until the mixture forms a soft and pliable dough.

Turn out on to a lightly floured surface and knead for approx 5 mins until smooth and free from cracks. Place in a lightly oiled bowl. Cover with a clean, plain tea towel and leave to prove in a warm place for 30-40 mins or until the dough has doubled in size.

Re-knead the dough, knock the dough with your knuckles until smooth and pliable, then divide into eight portions. Form each portion into a smooth round and arrange in the tin, placing seven round the edge with one in the middle. Cover with a tea towel and leave to rise in a warm place for 20-30 mins.

Brush with beaten egg, sprinkle with remaining cheese and the poppy and sesame seeds. Bake for 35-40 mins until risen and golden. When cooked the loaf will sound hollow if tapped on the base. Break into portions to serve. Best served warm.

Handy tips

Use a medium flavoured Cheddar cheese for best results. Try serving the bread as part of a Ploughman's snack at lunch or supper-time.

1. Place the yeast in a small bowl or jug with the sugar, and cream together until smooth

2. Mix in Parmesan cheese, 4 oz/100 g of the Cheddar cheese, crushed garlic, herbs and seasoning

3. Turn dough on to a lightly floured surface and knead for approx 5 mins until smooth and free from cracks

4. Re-knead dough, knock it with knuckles until pliable. Divide into eight portions. Form each portion into a smooth round

5. Arrange the rounds in the tin – seven round the edge and one in the middle. Cover with tea towel and leave to rise

6. Brush with beaten egg, sprinkle over remaining cheese, poppy and sesame seeds. Bake for 35-40 mins

Cottage Loaf

There's nothing quite like the aroma of freshly baked bread to welcome the family home after a busy day. The flavour and texture of home baked bread is unique, once tasted you're hooked. Make a double batch and freeze a loaf for another day.

Calories per portion: 212   **Serves 8**

1lb/450 g strong white flour
pinch of salt
2 tsp caster sugar
1 x ¼ oz/6 g sachet
   easy-blend yeast
½ oz/15 g butter or margarine
1 tbsp milk
butter to serve

Preheat the oven to Gas 8, 450°F, 230°C, 15 mins before baking the loaf. Sieve the flour into a large mixing bowl, stir in the salt, sugar and easy-blend yeast. Using your fingertips rub the fat into the flour until the mixture resembles fine breadcrumbs. Make a well in the centre of the dry ingredients then add approx ½ pint/300 ml tepid boiled water. Mix together using a fork or wooden spoon and then with your hands work to form a firm dough. Turn out on lightly floured surface and knead thoroughly for about 10 mins until the dough feels smooth and elastic.

Lightly oil a clean bowl then place the dough in the bowl, cover with a clean tea towel or piece of clearwrap and leave to rise in a warm place away from draughts for approx 1 hr or until the dough has doubled in size and springs back when pressed lightly with a floured finger.

Turn dough out on to a lightly floured surface and knock down. Knead again with the knuckles, flattening and stretching without tearing the dough to remove as many of the air bubbles as possible.

Once the dough feels really smooth and elastic cut off approx one third. Shape the larger piece into a smooth round then place on a lightly greased baking sheet. Take the other piece of dough and shape into a smaller round. Brush the top of the large round lightly with water then place the smaller round on top. Press down firmly. Dust your forefinger with flour then make an indent in the centre of the smaller round.

Cover the loaf with a clean tea towel then leave again to rise in a warm place away from draughts for approx 30 mins or until the dough springs back when pressed lightly with the finger.

Brush the loaf with a little milk then bake in the preheated oven for 20-25 mins or until cooked. To test if cooked, turn the loaf upside down and tap lightly on the base, it should sound hollow. Cool on a wire rack. Serve spread with butter.

Handy tip

If liked replace 6 oz/175 g of the white flour with strong wholemeal flour. Also try sprinkling the loaf with sesame or poppy seeds after brushing with the milk and before baking.

1. Sieve the flour into a mixing bowl, stir in the salt, sugar and easy-blend yeast, rub in the fat

2. Mix to a firm dough with tepid boiled water then knead on a lightly floured surface for approx 10 mins

3. After the dough has risen and doubled in size, turn out on to a lightly floured surface and knock down

4. Knead the dough until it feels smooth and elastic, knocking out as many of the air bubbles as possible

5. Cut off approx one third of the dough and then shape the larger piece into a round. Place on greased baking sheet

6. Shape the smaller piece of dough, brush the base of the loaf with water, place smaller round on top

FLORENTINES

Chopped glacé cherries, angelica, almonds, peel and sultanas in a wonderful toffee biscuit coated with rich dark chocolate... wicked? Yes, but spoil your family and friends with these delicious chewy treats.

Calories per portion: 97 **Makes 12**

- 1½ oz/40 g glacé cherries, chopped
- 1 oz/25 g angelica, chopped
- 2 oz/50 g butter or margarine
- 2 oz/50 g demerara sugar
- 1 tbsp golden syrup
- 1 oz/25 g mixed peel, chopped
- 2 oz/50 g sultanas, chopped
- 1½ oz/40 g flaked almonds, chopped
- 2 oz/50 g plain white flour, sifted
- 2 tbsp cream
- 6 oz/175 g plain chocolate

Preheat oven to Gas 4, 350°F, 180°C, 10 mins before baking. Lightly grease three baking sheets with oil. Wash and dry the glacé cherries and angelica and finely chop.

Heat butter or margarine with sugar and syrup, stirring occasionally until sugar has melted. Remove from heat, stir in chopped peel, sultanas and nuts. Stir flour into the mixture with the cream. Mix until blended.

Place small teaspoons of the mixture on to the greased baking sheets, allowing for the mixture to expand during cooking. Place on the centre shelf of the oven and cook for 8-10 mins or until the florentines are golden in colour. Remove from the oven and allow to cool for 1-2 mins. (It's quite all right if you bake one batch at a time – the mixture won't spoil if it's kept waiting a while.)

Then, with a round-bladed knife, carefully push the outside edges of each florentine towards the centre to make them as round as possible. Leave for a further 2-3 mins, or until they're just beginning to harden, then with a palette knife carefully transfer to a wire cooling rack. Leave until completely cold before decorating the bases with the melted chocolate.

Break the chocolate into small pieces and place in a small glass bowl over a pan of gently simmering water. Stir until melted and free from lumps. Coat the flat side of each florentine with a little melted chocolate. With the prongs of a fork, mark wavy lines across the chocolate and leave to set.

Store in an airtight tin layered with sheets of greaseproof paper. Florentines will keep for at least a week. They do not freeze well.

Handy tip

Make tiny florentines, by putting very small amounts on to baking sheets. Cook for 4-6 mins. Use as petit fours.

1. Wash and dry cherries and angelica. Chop with sultanas, almonds and peel

2. Melt fat, demerara sugar and syrup in a small pan and stir until dissolved

3. Put teaspoonfuls on to a greased baking sheet, allowing room to spread

CAKES & BAKES

4. Allow florentines to stand for 1-2 mins then transfer to a wire cooling rack

5. When cold, coat the flat side of each florentine with the melted chocolate

6. Finally, using the prongs of a fork, make a decorative pattern on the base

HOME-MADE BISCUITS

Welcome the kids home with a tray of home-made biscuits. It's really easy to do with this recipe. Make the dough in advance and leave it chilling in the fridge then just shape and bake the biscuits as and when you need them.

Calories per portion: 97 MAKES APPROX 60

1. Cream the fat and sugar in two bowls until pale and fluffy, add egg, then the flour and cocoa or vanilla

2. For pinwheels, roll the chocolate and vanilla doughs together, as for a Swiss roll. Cut thin slices, place on baking sheet

3. For chequerboards, arrange equal lengths of chocolate and white doughs to give a chequered effect

10 oz/300 g butter
  or margarine
10 oz/300 g caster sugar
2 eggs, size 3
15 oz/425 g plain white
  flour, sieved
1 oz/25 g cocoa powder, sieved
½ tsp vanilla essence
few glacé cherries, sliced
2 oz/50 g vanilla-flavoured
  butter cream
extra caster sugar and icing
  sugar for dredging
1 oz/25 g plain chocolate, melted

Preheat oven to Gas 5, 375°F, 190°C, 10 mins before baking the biscuits. Lightly oil three baking sheets. (You will find it easier to make the dough in two separate bowls so that the proportions are correct.)

In each bowl cream together 5 oz/150 g of fat and sugar until pale and fluffy. Lightly whisk the eggs and gradually beat into each mixture. Into one bowl stir in 7 oz/200 g of the plain flour and the 1 oz/25 g of cocoa powder. Mix well until the mixture forms a soft dough. Wrap in baking parchment and chill for 30 mins. Add the remaining flour and vanilla essence to the other bowl, mix ingredients together to form a soft dough, wrap then chill for at least 30 mins.

After shaping, chill the biscuits for 30 mins before baking for 8-10 mins. Remove from the oven and cool for 1 min before transferring to a wire cooling rack.

To make pinwheels, roll out an equal amount of both doughs on a lightly floured surface and cut out two oblongs, ensuring they are the same thickness and size. Place the chocolate dough on top of the vanilla dough and roll up as for a Swiss roll. Cut out thin slices and place on baking sheet. Chill before baking.

To make chequerboards, roll out equal amounts of both doughs to form two oblongs, cut each in half lengthways. Place one white and chocolate length side by side then place the remaining chocolate oblong on top of the white oblong and the remaining white oblong on the chocolate. Press lightly together. Cut into thin slices and place on baking sheets. Chill then bake.

To make garlands, with the white dough, use your hands to form eight small balls about the size of a pea. Place together on a baking sheet forming a circle. Cut very thin slices from a glacé cherry and place in between the joins. Dredge lightly with caster sugar, chill then bake.

To make chocolate dodgers, roll the chocolate dough out on a lightly floured surface to approx ¼ in/6 mm thickness. Cut out equal amounts of 2 in/5 cm rounds with a plain cutter. Using a ½ in/1.25 cm plain cutter, cut out the centres of half the rounds. Place on baking sheet and chill then bake. Once cold sandwich together, with the butter cream, one plain biscuit and one with the hole. Dredge lightly with icing sugar.

To make chocolate twists, roll out the white dough to an oblong ¼ in/6 mm thick. Cut out thin slices approx ¼ in/6 mm wide. Twist two strips together then place on a baking sheet. Dredge lightly with caster sugar and chill. When cooked and cold dip both ends in the melted chocolate and leave until set.

HANDY TIP

The dough can be made and left in the fridge then small batches can be baked as required.

4. For garlands, roll out eight small balls, place on baking sheet in a circle with sliced cherries in joins

5. For chocolate dodgers, roll out chocolate dough and cut an even number of rounds with a plain cutter

6. To make chocolate twists, roll out vanilla-flavoured dough, cut into thin strips and twist two strips together

Viennese Fingers

Tempt the whole family with these delicious biscuits. Filled with a vanilla buttercream and dipped in plain chocolate, they just melt in the mouth. They taste so good you'll have to hide them away if you want any left for tea-time.

Calories per portion: 438 | Makes 10 biscuits

7 oz/200 g unsalted butter or margarine
2 oz/50 g icing sugar, sifted
½ oz/15 g cornflour
4 oz/100 g self-raising flour
4 oz/100 g plain flour
1 tsp vanilla essence

FOR THE BUTTERCREAM FILLING:
3 oz/75 g butter or margarine
6 oz/175 g icing sugar, sifted
½ tsp vanilla essence
5 oz/150 g plain chocolate

Preheat oven to Gas 4, 350°F, 180°C, 10 mins before baking. Lightly grease two baking sheets. Cream the fat with the sifted icing sugar until soft and fluffy, then beat in the cornflour. Sift both flours together then gradually beat into the creamed mixture until thoroughly blended. Beat in the vanilla essence. The mixture should be stiff, but smooth, and free from lumps.

Spoon into a medium-sized piping bag fitted with a large star nozzle. Pipe 3 in/7.5 cm lengths on to the greased baking sheets, allowing room for expansion. You may find it easier to pipe the mixture if the piping bag is only half filled as this will enable you to put more pressure on to the bag as you pipe.

Bake on the centre shelf of the oven for 15-20 mins or until the biscuits are cooked and light golden brown. If necessary turn the baking sheet halfway round during cooking time for even baking. Remove from the oven and allow to cool for a few minutes before carefully transferring to a wire cooling rack. Leave until completely cold.

To make buttercream, cream the butter or margarine with the sifted icing sugar until soft and fluffy. Beat in the vanilla essence. Place to one side.

Break the chocolate into pieces and put into a small bowl over a pan of gently simmering water and allow to melt, stirring occasionally. Dip each end of the biscuit into the melted chocolate, then leave to set on sheets of greaseproof paper.

When the chocolate has completely set, spoon the buttercream into the piping bag. Using a large star nozzle, pipe the buttercream down the centre of one biscuit. Place another biscuit on top and press lightly together. Continue until all the biscuits have been sandwiched together in pairs.

HANDY TIPS

Take care when handling the biscuits. They are so 'short' they do tend to break very easily. Vary the flavour by using a chocolate buttercream, or by adding lemon or orange rind to the biscuit mixture with rind and juice to the buttercream.

1. Cream the butter or margarine with the sifted icing sugar until fluffy

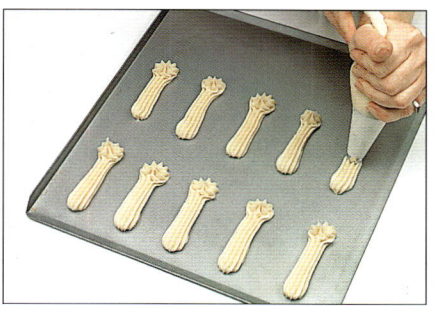

2. Pipe 3 in/7.5 cm lengths of mixture on to lightly greased baking sheets

3. When biscuits are cooked, cool slightly, then place on a wire cooling rack

4. Dip biscuits into the melted chocolate, leave to set on greaseproof paper

5. Fold the piping bag down over your hand, spoon in prepared buttercream

6. Pipe the buttercream on to the biscuits and carefully sandwich together

GINGERBREAD PEOPLE

Treat the kids with these delicious crunchy biscuits. Rich with honey and syrup, they're easy to make and ready in minutes. And why not pop one into a lunch box for a tasty surprise.

Calories per portion: 286 **MAKES 14**

1-2 tsp vegetable oil
12 oz/350 g plain flour
1 level tsp bicarbonate of soda
2 level tsp ground ginger
4 oz/100 g block margarine
4 oz/100 g light soft brown sugar
2 level tsp clear honey
2 tbsp golden syrup
1 egg, size 3
few currants
3 oz/75 g icing sugar

Preheat the oven to Gas 5, 375°F, 190°C, 10 mins before baking. Lightly grease three baking sheets with the oil. Sieve the flour, bicarbonate of soda and ground ginger into a mixing bowl. Add the margarine, then rub into the flour until the mixture resembles fine breadcrumbs. Stir in the soft brown sugar and mix well.

Place the honey and syrup in a small pan and heat through gently, stirring until it is thoroughly blended. Take care not to allow the mixture to boil. Remove from the heat. Beat the egg, then beat into the warmed syrup mixture until thoroughly incorporated. Stir into the flour mixture and mix to form a soft dough. Knead lightly until smooth.

Place on a lightly floured surface (don't use too much flour as this will affect the proportions and the finished result). Roll out the dough to ¼ in/6 mm thickness then, using cutters, cut out the gingerbread people. Place on the greased baking sheets and arrange two currants on each to represent the eyes. Bake in the oven for 10-12 mins or until cooked. Cool slightly. Then transfer to wire cooling racks until cold.

Sieve icing sugar then mix with about 1½ tbsp tepid boiled water until a smooth piping consistency is formed. Place in a piping bag fitted with a small plain piping nozzle. Carefully pipe along the outline of the gingerbread men and pipe a tie or buttons, too. Pipe an apron on the gingerbread women. Store in an airtight tin.

HANDY TIPS

Gingerbread people cutters can be bought from some supermarkets, kitchen shops and department stores. If preferred, draw shapes on a clean piece of card and cut round shapes.
These biscuits are really easy to make, and if you keep an eye on your kids while they're handling the warmed honey and syrup, they make a super, fun piece of cooking for them to do!

1. Sieve flour, bicarbonate of soda and ground ginger into a large mixing bowl

2. Add margarine to flour, then rub in until mixture resembles fine breadcrumbs

3. Add the warmed ingredients to the flour, then mix to form a soft dough

CAKES & BAKES

4. Knead, then roll out the dough on a floured surface to ¼ in/6 mm thickness

5. Using gingerbread cutters, cut out the dough and place on baking sheets

6. Arrange the currants on the gingerbread people to represent their eyes

Cookie Biscuits

Quick and easy to bake, you can't beat home-made biscuits! The varieties you can make are endless – the choice is yours. And they taste so delicious, with a melt-in-the-mouth texture, you'll have to hide them to save any for tea.

Calories per portion: 160 **Makes 35**

- 10 oz/300 g butter or margarine
- 1 lb/450 g plain flour
- 9 oz/250 g caster sugar
- 1 egg, size 3, beaten
- 2 oz/50 g chocolate cooking chips
- 2 tbsp raspberry jam
- ½ tsp almond essence
- 2 oz/50 g chopped almonds
- 2 oz/50 g glacé cherries
- grated rind of ½ orange
- 1 tsp ground cinnamon
- 2 tbsp porridge oats

Preheat oven to Gas 5, 375°F, 190°C, 10 mins before baking. Lightly grease five baking sheets. Rub the butter or margarine into the sieved flour and sugar with your fingers, until the fat has been thoroughly incorporated. Bind together with sufficient beaten egg to give a stiff but pliable dough. On a clean surface, knead the dough until smooth then divide into five equal portions.

Into one portion add chocolate chips and knead until the chocolate chips are thoroughly distributed throughout the dough. Form into small balls about the size of a walnut and place well apart on lightly greased baking sheet.

With another portion of dough, again form into small balls the size of a walnut. Roll round in the hands until smooth then place well apart on a baking sheet. Make a small hole in the centre, ensuring you don't go right through to the base. Spoon a small amount of raspberry jam in the centre.

Into a further portion of dough knead ½ tsp of almond essence. Place chopped almonds in a small bowl then form dough into small balls about the size of a walnut and roll in the almonds. Place on to greased baking sheet.

Wash and dry the glacé cherries then chop finely. Knead the cherries into another portion of dough. Form this dough into balls and place on to greased baking sheet.

Into the last remaining portion of the dough, add the grated orange rind and cinnamon. Knead well. Form into balls and roll in the porridge oats. Place on to greased baking sheet and sprinkle tops with a few more porridge oats.

Bake in the oven for 15-20 mins or until the biscuits are lightly golden brown. Remove from the oven, leave to cool for 3 mins before transferring to a wire cooling rack. When cold, store in an airtight tin.

Handy Tip

You can vary the biscuits according to taste. Try using lemon curd instead of jam, raisins or currants instead of the chocolate chips, chopped walnuts in place of the cherries. Or use a different spice such as ginger, mixed spice, nutmeg or ground mace. All are delicious!

1. Mix fat into sieved flour and sugar. Bind together with beaten egg

2. Place on to a clean surface then knead the dough gently until smooth

3. Divide dough into equal portions. Knead the chocolate chips into one portion

CAKES & BAKES 83

4. Form another portion into balls, place on baking sheet. Make hole, add jam

5. After flavouring a portion with almond essence, roll the balls in nuts

6. Chop cherries finely, add to dough portion. Knead then roll into balls

CHOCOLATE CHEESECAKE

For a change serve this delicious rich and creamy chocolate cheesecake that's encased in a light chocolate pastry. Eat it warm by itself or for an extra indulgence with lashings of whipped cream.

Calories per portion: 401　　　　　　　　　　Serves 12

FOR THE PASTRY:
8 oz/225 g plain flour
2 tbsp cocoa powder
4 tbsp icing sugar
5 oz/150 g butter or margarine

FOR THE FILLING:
3 eggs, size 3, separated
4 oz/100 g caster sugar
8 oz/225 g curd cheese
2 oz/50 g ground almonds
10 fl oz/300 ml double cream
1½ oz/40 g cocoa powder, sifted
1 tbsp rum
icing sugar and cocoa powder
  to dust

Preheat oven to Gas 4, 350°F, 180°C, 10 mins before baking. Lightly grease a 9 in/23 cm loose-bottomed tin. Sieve 2 oz/50 g plain flour into a small bowl and remaining flour into a larger bowl. Sieve the cocoa and icing sugar into the larger bowl. Add 1 oz/25 g of the fat to the 2 oz/50 g of flour and add the remaining fat to the larger bowl. Rub both amounts of fat into flours until the mixtures resemble fine breadcrumbs. Bind together with cold water to form two soft but not sticky doughs. Wrap and chill in fridge for at least 1 hr. Roll out the chocolate pastry 2 in/5 cm larger than the tin and use to line the base and sides. Chill while preparing the cheesecake filling.

Make the filling by whisking the egg yolks and caster sugar together until pale, thick and creamy. Whisk in the curd cheese then the ground almonds, cream and finally the cocoa powder. Stir in the rum and mix until thoroughly blended.

Whisk the egg whites until stiff and standing in peaks then using a metal spoon, carefully fold into the mixture ensuring that it is thoroughly incorporated. Pour into the pastry-lined tin and tap lightly on a surface to ensure there are no air bubbles.

Roll out the plain pastry on a lightly floured surface and cut into thin strips. Dampen edges lightly with a little water then arrange across the top of the cheesecake forming a lattice pattern. Place on a baking sheet then bake in the oven for 1-1½ hrs or until firm to the touch. Remove from the oven and allow the cheesecake to stand 10 mins before removing from the tin. Dredge with icing sugar and cocoa powder.

HANDY TIP

If liked, vary the flavour: try substituting the rum with 1 tbsp cooled, strong black coffee or 1 tbsp Tia Maria.

1. Rub fat into the flour and cocoa until mixture resembles fine breadcrumbs. Bind together with cold water

2. Roll out chocolate pastry. Use to line the base and sides of tin then chill while preparing the cheesecake filling

3. Whisk egg yolks and caster sugar until thick, whisk in curd cheese, almonds and cocoa powder. Stir in rum

4. Whisk the egg whites until stiff and standing in peaks then fold into the cheesecake mixture. Mix well

5. Pour the prepared filling into the chilled pastry-lined tin, tap lightly on the surface to remove any air bubbles

6. Roll out the plain pastry and cut into thin strips. Arrange in a lattice pattern across the top of the mixture

Butterscotch Tart

Crisp, light pastry that melts in the mouth. Flavoured with just a hint of cinnamon and filled with a rich buttery centre that's wickedly delicious, try making this special treat.

Calories per portion: 325

Serves 10

- 6 oz/175 g plain flour
- 4 oz/100 g butter or margarine
- 1 tsp ground cinnamon
- 1 tbsp caster sugar
- 1 egg yolk, size 1

FOR THE FILLING:
- 4 oz/100 g soft dark brown sugar
- 2 heaped tbsp cornflour
- ½ tsp salt
- ¾ pint/450 ml semi-skimmed milk
- 1 egg, size 1, beaten
- 2 oz/50 g butter
- ½ tsp vanilla essence
- ¼ pint/150 ml whipping cream and chocolate curls to decorate

Preheat oven to Gas 6, 400°F, 200°C, 15 mins before baking. Place the flour into a mixing bowl. Add the butter or margarine, with the ground cinnamon and caster sugar. Add the egg yolk with 2-3 tsp cold water. Using the fingers, work the mixture into a smooth, but not sticky, dough. Knead lightly on a floured surface, wrap and chill in the fridge for 30 mins.

Roll out on a lightly floured surface and use to line an 8 in/20.5 cm fluted flan ring. (Place the flan ring on a baking sheet if the ring has no base.) Take care not to split the pastry, and ensure that the sides are of uniform thickness.

Place a sheet of tin foil or greaseproof paper and baking beans in the base and bake blind for 10-15 mins. Remove the foil or paper and baking beans and cook the flan for a further 5-10 mins, or until pale golden and cooked completely. Leave on one side to cool while preparing filling.

Place the soft dark brown sugar, the cornflour and salt into a pan and gradually mix in milk to form a smooth paste. Place over a gentle heat, cook, stirring throughout until thick and free from any lumps. Turn off the heat and gradually beat in the egg. Return saucepan to the heat. Cook gently for a further 2-3 mins, stirring continuously. Remove from the heat, then beat in the butter and vanilla essence. Beat until smooth and glossy. Pour into the flan case and smooth the top. Leave to cool, then chill in the fridge for at least 2-3 hrs before decorating.

Whip the cream until thick, place in a piping bag fitted with a star nozzle and pipe a pattern on top of the tart. Decorate with the chocolate curls

Handy tip

If the butterscotch filling is a little lumpy, either sieve it or give it a whizz in a food processor or blender after cooking, then add the butter and vanilla essence.

1. Place flour and butter or margarine in a bowl. Add cinnamon and sugar

2. Line a flan ring with pastry then foil. Bake blind for 10-15 mins

3. Place sugar and cornflour in pan. Blend in milk to form a smooth paste

4. Place over a gentle heat. Stir continuously until thick and free of lumps

5. Turn off heat and beat in egg. Return to heat, cook for 2-3 mins.

6. Pour filling into the cooked pastry case, smooth top. Leave until cold

Gateau St. Honore

This choux pastry gâteau, called the 'masterpiece of pâtisserie' is named after St. Honorius, patron saint of bakers. It is filled with delicious custard, then topped with caramel and chocolate curls.

Calories per portion: 356 — Serves 10

1. For the pâte sucrée, work the sugar, butter and egg yolks into the flour

2. Beat the eggs, a little at a time, into the cooled choux pastry mixture

3. Pipe choux pastry into small mounds on a lightly greased baking sheet

FOR THE PATE SUCREE:
4 oz/100 g plain flour
pinch of salt
2 oz/50 g caster sugar
2 oz/50 g butter, cut into cubes
2 egg yolks, size 3

FOR THE CHOUX PASTRY:
4 oz/100 g butter
5 oz/150 g plain flour, sieved
4 eggs, size 3

FOR THE CREME PATISSIERE:
2 eggs, size 3
2 oz/50 g caster sugar
2 tbsp flour
2 tbsp cornflour
½ pint/300 ml milk
few drops vanilla essence

FOR THE CARAMEL:
6 tbsp granulated sugar
chocolate curls and icing sugar to decorate

Preheat the oven to Gas 6, 400°F, 200°C, 15 mins before baking. Sieve the flour for the pâte sucrée on to a clean work surface with the salt. Make a well in the centre and add the sugar, butter and egg yolks. Work into the flour with the fingertips to form a smooth pastry. Cover in clearwrap and chill for 1 hr. On a floured surface, roll out the pâte sucrée into a 9 in/23 cm circle. Place on a greased baking sheet and prick the base with a fork.

To make the choux pastry, melt butter in a saucepan with ½ pint/300 ml water. Bring to boil. Remove from heat and add sieved flour to pan. Beat well until mixture becomes glossy and forms a ball. Don't overbeat mixture. Cool for 5 mins. Beat in eggs, a little at a time, bringing the mixture back to its original consistency after each addition. Place the choux pastry in a piping bag fitted with a large plain nozzle. Pipe a circle around the edge of the pastry about 2 in/5 cm in width. Lightly grease another baking sheet and using the remaining choux pastry, pipe 14-18 walnut-sized mounds. Place both baking sheets in oven for 15-20 mins, or until the choux pastry is risen and golden. Remove from the oven and leave until cold.

To make the crème pâtissière, whisk eggs and sugar together until pale and thick. Place flour and cornflour in a bowl and blend to a smooth paste with a little milk. Heat remaining milk in a pan until almost boiling. Pour over egg mixture, stirring constantly. Return custard to pan and stir in the cornflour mixture. Stir over a low heat until the mixture coats the back of a wooden spoon, then add the vanilla essence. Cover with a damp sheet of greaseproof paper and cool. When cooled, place in a piping bag fitted with a plain potato nozzle. Make a hole in the base of each choux bun and pipe in a little crème pâtissière.

To make the caramel, place sugar in a pan with 6 tbsp water. Heat, stirring occasionally, until the sugar dissolves. Increase heat and boil until mixture turns golden. Remove from the heat and place base of pan in a bowl of cold water. Dip base and top of each choux bun into the liquid caramel.

Arrange the buns around choux ring. Fill gâteau with remaining crème pâtissière. Decorate with chocolate curls, dust with icing sugar and serve.

HANDY TIPS

Assemble the gâteau no more than ½ hr before serving. For accurate measuring always use measuring spoons, available from all kitchen ware shops and departmental stores.

4. Heat crème pâtissière until it coats the back of a wooden spoon

5. Dip base and top of buns into the caramel and arrange around choux ring

6. Fill the centre of the gâteau with the remaining crème pâtissière

TREACLE TART

Can you remember the gooey treacle tart that your grandma used to make? Well, we'll bring these memories flooding back with this super easy recipe – you'll just love it! To make it extra special we've added a hint of ginger.

Calories per portion: 476

SERVES 8

FOR PASTRY:
12 oz/350 g plain flour
3 oz/75 g margarine
3 oz/75 g white fat or lard

FOR FILLING:
8 oz/225 g golden syrup
1½ oz/40 g butter or margarine
1½ oz/40 g white breadcrumbs
grated rind of 1 large lemon
1 oz/25 g stem ginger, finely chopped (optional)
1 egg, size 3, beaten

Preheat oven to Gas 6, 400°F, 200°C, 15 mins before baking. Sift flour into a mixing bowl, then rub fat in with the fingertips until mixture resembles fine breadcrumbs. Mix to a soft and pliable dough with 5-6 tbsp cold water. Knead the pastry on a lightly floured surface until it is smooth and free from cracks.

Roll out to ¼ in/6 mm thick and use to line a 9 in/23 cm pie plate. Prick base lightly with a fork. Roll out trimmings and cut out eight ¼ in/6 mm wide strips with a pastry wheel, and with a ½ in/1.25 cm pastry cutter stamp out approx 45 rounds. Chill pastry-lined plate while preparing filling:

Melt syrup and butter or margarine in a small pan. Stir in breadcrumbs, lemon rind and stem ginger (if using). Draw off heat, cool slightly then mix in the beaten egg.

Spoon the treacle filling into the centre of the pastry-lined plate, allowing the filling to come to within 1 in/2.5 cm of the edge of the plate. Dampen edges with a little water then arrange pastry strips across the tart to give a lattice effect as illustrated.

Dampen the little pastry rounds with a little water and fix into position round edge of pastry, as illustrated. Knock edges together with a round-bladed knife. If you like, brush the pastry with a little beaten egg to glaze.

Bake in the preheated oven for 20-25 mins or until the pastry is golden brown and cooked. Serve warm with custard or cream.

HANDY TIPS

As an alternative to ginger, try 1½ tsp ground cinnamon or mixed spice.
For added crunch add 2 oz/50 g toasted chopped almonds to the filling before cooking.

1. Rub fat into the flour until the mixture resembles fine breadcrumbs

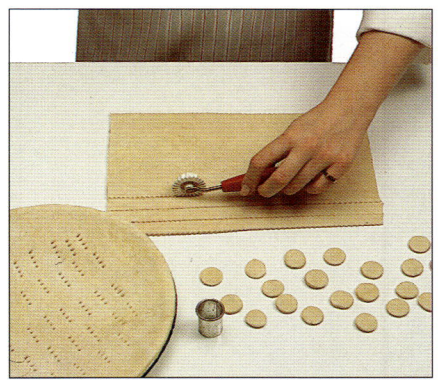

2. Line plate and cut the trimmings into lattice strips and small rounds

3. Melt syrup and butter or margarine in a small pan over a low heat

4. Add breadcrumbs, lemon rind and chopped ginger, leave to cool slightly

5. Spoon filling on to pastry-lined plate to within 1 in/2.5 cm of edge

6. Dampen edges of pastry then lay the pastry strips across in a lattice effect

FRUIT SAVARIN

A delicious rich yeast cake, soaked in a rum syrup then filled with a wonderful mixture of fresh summer fruits. Make it the day before and allow the syrup to really soak through to the sponge.

Calories per portion: 447

SERVES 6

- 8 oz/225 g strong plain flour
- 1 tbsp easy-blend yeast
- 6 fl oz/175 ml milk
- ½ level tsp salt
- 2 oz/50 g caster sugar
- 4 eggs, size 3
- 4 oz/100 g softened butter
- 4 tbsp clear honey
- 3-4 tbsp dark rum
- 1 small ripe ogen melon
- 8 oz/225 g strawberries
- 4 oz/100 g raspberries
- 4 oz/100 g black grapes, preferably seedless
- cream to serve

Preheat oven to Gas 6, 400°F, 200°C, 15 mins before baking. Well butter a 9 in/23 cm savarin mould. Sift 2 oz/50 g of the flour into a large mixing bowl and sprinkle in the easy-blend yeast. Warm the milk to blood heat (to test for blood heat the milk should feel hot, not boiling, when a clean finger is dipped in) then add to the flour and yeast mixture and mix together. Cover with a piece of clearwrap or clean tea towel. Leave in a warm place, away from draughts for 20 mins or until frothy.

Sift the remaining flour and the salt into the yeast mixture with the sugar. Beat the eggs together then add to the flour, and beat to a smooth batter. Cut the butter into small squares then add to batter, beating until the butter is incorporated. Pour into the buttered mould, cover with clearwrap or a clean tea towel and leave to rise for a further 50-55 mins. The tin should be half full before being left to rise.

Bake on centre shelf for 25 mins or until cooked. The savarin should start to shrink away slightly from the sides of the tin. Remove from the oven, carefully slip a round-bladed knife around the sides of tin to loosen then invert on a wire cooling rack. Leave the savarin until cold.

Heat the honey with 3 tablespoons of water, bring to the boil, boil for 2 mins to form a syrup. Stir in the rum.

Place savarin on a plate standing over a wire cooling rack, then spoon over the syrup until thoroughly moistened. Transfer to serving plate.

Cut melon in half, discard seeds and either use a melon ball cutter, make melon balls or peel and cut into small cubes. Hull and rinse strawberries and raspberries. Wash and dry grapes. Mix fruits together and pile into centre of savarin. Serve with cream.

HANDY TIP

The base can be made in advance and frozen or kept for up to one week in an airtight container. The drier the savarin the more syrup you should use.

1. Add yeast to 2 oz/50 g of the flour, mix in the milk and leave for approx 20 mins until frothy

2. Sift the remaining flour and salt into the frothy yeast mixture then stir in the caster sugar. Mix well together

3. Beat the eggs together, then gradually mix into the flour mixture, beat well to form a smooth batter

CAKES & BAKES   93

4. Cut the butter into small squares, add to the batter and beat until the butter is incorporated

5. Pour the batter into the buttered 9 in/23 cm savarin mould, smooth top, bake in the preheated oven

6. Turn the cooked savarin out on to a wire cooling rack then spoon syrup over whilst still warm

Frangipane Tart

Melt-in-the-mouth pastry topped with a light lemon-flavoured sponge and sprinkled with flaked almonds. This Frangipane Tart is so simple to make! Serve it hot with custard for pud, or cold for tea-time.

Calories per portion: 466 **Cuts into 12 slices**

FOR THE PASTRY:
- 10 oz/300 g plain flour
- 7 oz/200 g unsalted butter or block margarine
- 1 oz/25 g caster sugar
- 1 egg yolk, size 3
- grated rind ½ lemon

FOR THE FILLING:
- 12 oz/340 g jar raspberry jam
- 4 oz/100 g butter or margarine
- 4½ oz/120 g caster sugar
- 2 eggs, size 3
- 2 oz/50 g ground almonds
- grated rind and juice of 1 lemon
- 4 oz/100 g self-raising flour, sifted
- 2 oz/50 g flaked almonds

Preheat oven to Gas 6, 400°F, 200°C, 15 mins before baking. Sift flour into a large mixing bowl. Cut the fat into cubes and add to the flour with the sugar, egg yolk and lemon rind.

Then using your hands mix together, adding 2-3 tbsp of cold water to form a smooth but not sticky dough. Knead on a lightly floured surface until smooth and free from cracks. Wrap in clearwrap and chill in the fridge for 20 mins before rolling out and lining a 10 in/25.5 cm fluted flan tin.

Spoon the jam into the centre then spread evenly over the base. Chill while preparing rest of the filling.

Cream butter or margarine with 4 oz/100 g of the sugar until light and fluffy. Beat the eggs then gradually beat into the mixture with the ground almonds. Fold in the lemon rind and juice, and sifted flour. Add 2-3 tbsp of cooled boiled water to give a soft dropping consistency. Place in centre of lined pastry case over the jam and spread evenly, ensuring that the jam is completely covered. Sprinkle top of the tart with the flaked almonds.

Bake on the centre shelf in the preheated oven for 15 mins. Reduce oven temperature to Gas 4, 350°F, 180°C, and continue to cook for a further 20-30 mins or until the filling is cooked and golden brown.

The filling should spring back when touched lightly with a clean finger. Remove from oven, sprinkle with remaining caster sugar and leave until cool. Remove from flan tin and place on serving plate.

HANDY TIPS

You can vary the flavour by replacing the raspberry jam with another jam or lemon curd. Alter the texture as well as the flavour by using apricots. Drain a 14 oz/397 g can of apricots, place over pastry case. Replace the lemon rind and juice in the sponge with 1 tsp almond essence. Spread filling over and sprinkle with almonds, and bake. Or try a different topping – omit almonds on top and bake. Allow to cool then cover top with 6 oz/175 g prepared glacé icing. Leave to set before cutting.

1. Carefully wrap pastry around rolling pin and gently place in position over flan tin

2. Gently press pastry into sides of flan tin, ensuring that there are no air pockets

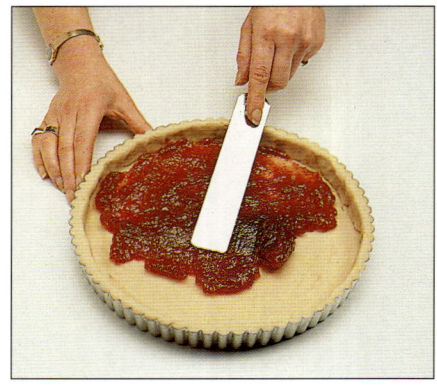

3. Spread jam evenly over base of pastry-lined tin. Leave to chill, prepare filling

CAKES & BAKES

4. Cream butter or margarine with sugar, gradually beat in eggs and almonds

5. Spread prepared filling evenly over jam in flan, ensuring that jam is covered

6. Sprinkle top with the flaked almonds, then bake in the preheated oven

Index

Angel food cake 26

Battenburg cake 6
Biscuits:
    Cookie biscuits 82
    Florentines 74
    Gingerbread people 80
    Home-made biscuits 76
    Viennese fingers 78
Bread:
    Cottage loaf 72
    Herb and cheese loaf 70
    Panettone 44
    Stollen 32
Brownies, chocolate 64
Buns:
    Chelsea buns 54
    Tea cakes 62
Butterscotch tart 86

Caraque, chocolate 40
Cheese:
    Herb and cheese loaf 70
Cheesecake, chocolate 84
Chelsea buns 54
Cherry and date cake 8
Chocolate:
    Chocolate brownies 64
    Chocolate cake 20
    Chocolate caraque 40
    Chocolate cheesecake 84
    Chocolate mousse cake 34

Choux pastry gâteau 88
Christmas cake 30
Cookie biscuits 82
Cottage loaf 72
Cream gâteau 36
Croissants 68
Crumpets 56

Danish pastries 60
Date:
    Cherry and date cake 8
Devil's food cake 38
Doughnuts 52
Dundee cake 12

Eccles cakes 48

Florentines 74
Frangipane tart 94
Fruit savarin 92
Fruity buns 62

Gâteau:
    Cream gâteau 36
    Gâteau St. Honore 88
Genoa cake 16
Gingerbread: 50
    Gingerbread house 42
    Gingerbread people 80

Herb and cheese loaf 70
Home-made biscuits 76

Mince pies 58
Mincemeat 58

Panettone 44
Passion cake 28
Pastries, Danish 60

Sachertorte 40
Savarin, fruit 92
Shortcakes, strawberry 66
Simnel cake 24
Stollen 32
Strawberry:
    Strawberry shortcakes 66
    Strawberry tarts 46
Swiss roll 10

Tarts:
    Butterscotch tart 86
    Frangipane tart 94
    Strawberry tarts 46
    Treacle tart 90
Tea cakes 62
Treacle tart 90

Victoria sandwich 18
Viennese fingers 78

Walnut cake 14

Yule log 22

Acknowledgements

All photography by John Elliot.
Except for: Genoa Cake, Stollen, Cream Gâteau, Chelsea Buns,
Danish Pastries and Baked Chocolate Cheesecake by David Armstrong.
Chocolate Caraque Cake, Tea Cakes, Croissants, Cottage Loaf and Homemade Biscuits by Karl Adamson.
Gingerbread House and Herb and Cheese Loaf by Ken Field.
Panettone by Ian 'O' Leary and Chocolate Brownies by Clive Streeter.

Gina Steer would like to thank Kathryn Hawkins and Jenny Brightman for their help in
assisting in some of the photography, styling and recipe testing.